a
beautiful
disaster

a
beautiful
disaster

finding hope
in the midst of brokenness

marlena graves

BrazosPress
a division of Baker Publishing Group
Grand Rapids, Michigan

© 2014 by Marlena Graves

Published by Brazos Press
a division of Baker Publishing Group
P.O. Box 6287, Grand Rapids, MI 49516-6287
www.brazospress.com

Printed in the United States of America

Library of Congress Cataloging-in-Publication Data is on file at the Library of Congress, Washington, DC.

ISBN 978-1-58743-341-2 (pbk.)

14 15 16 17 18 19 20   7 6 5 4 3 2 1

contents

foreword by john ortberg and laura ortberg turner   vii

part 1
this wilderness life

1. the way of the desert and beautiful souls 3
2. who am i? 11
3. to your cell for goodness's sake 27
4. loved into resurrection 45
5. testing and temptation 63
6. careless in the care of God 79
7. waiting around for God 95
8. the death of a dream 111
9. the God who sees me 127

part 2
wilderness gifts

10. weak and wise athletes of God 145
11. trembling in fear and adoration 161
12. children in the kingdom of God 177
13. a human being fully alive 195

notes 205

foreword

It is hard to imagine a more trustworthy guide in the wilderness than the author of the book you now have in your hands. Marlena Graves has been a friend of mine (Laura) for several years now, and the gentle wisdom I see in her is borne of the same long and painful winds that shape the hollow canyons of desert stone.

This is the kind of book the church needs now. Living in an age of easy distractions and constant comparison can result in a sort of nice numbness, a feeling that I'm all right and everything else is all right. Our worlds, able to expand with the click of a mouse, have never been smaller or more centered on ourselves. We are separated not only from other people but also from God and ourselves. This separation—this loss of integrity and wholeness—is a source of great grief in our lives.

Marlena's is the story of a faith rooted in crisis from a young age. Raised in poverty and amid great instability, she retreated into her imagination when things around her were out of control, which was often. She writes at one point of reading Genesis in her room in her family's trailer, walking behind Adam and Eve in the garden, inserting herself into the story of God at work in the world. The practice of *lectio divina* done, unknowingly, by a child.

In the words of Dallas Willard, a mentor and friend to both Marlena and me (John), "Spiritual formation in the tradition of Jesus Christ is the process of transformation of the inmost dimension of the human being, the heart, which is the same as the spirit or will. It is being formed (really, transformed) in such a way that its natural expression comes to be the deeds of Christ done in the power of Christ."[1] Understanding spiritual formation this way—as a manner of development in which our hearts become more like Christ's—is central to understanding the human condition. We do not become "new creations" overnight, by praying the right prayer or believing the right things. God makes us and renews us constantly and with our cooperation. This book takes that process seriously, reminding us that God does not take us to the wilderness to leave us, but dwells with us even in the most painful of landscapes.

The wilderness can take many different forms. Inspired by Jesus's command in Matthew 19:21 to "sell your possessions, and give the money to the poor," the desert fathers and mothers moved to the Egyptian desert to live alone or in small groups. Their lives were austere, but the wilderness was the place of their choosing. My own (Laura) wilderness experiences have been mostly of the unchosen variety, time spent paralyzed by anxiety and fear of the future, uncertainty and powerlessness looming like a Scylla and Charybdis from which I could never be free. Others have been brought to the wilderness in deep despair and have hoped the sands and the time would act as smoothing agents, hewing the rough edges of pain.

Some people spend their lives in the desert; some people are rarely there. The things that take us to the desert are varied. We may be there for a week or for years; we may be devastated or full of boredom; we may be alone or in great company.

But here's what we've come to learn: time in the desert prepares us for more time in the desert. Whether we remain there is beside the point; the point is the person we become when we are there.

One of the foundational questions this book addresses is our understanding of God. When we think of God, what and who do we understand God to be? I (Laura) have no trouble believing God to exist or be good, but I wonder whether God is truly close, whether God really wants to be a part of my life or if he is content to keep a watchful eye from far away. I cringe when people say they prayed for God to heal them from a cold or find the right parking place, but there is something of that intimacy that I envy too. For me (John), my early doubts were intellectualized. If God existed, I believed him to be near and good, but it was hard for me to trust someone with whom I could not use my senses to interact.

These are only two images of God that fall short of the whole; there are as many understandings of God as there are people on earth. But the great gift of this book is the search for a whole image of God. Wholeness, in this case, necessarily entails mystery—"What no eye has seen, nor ear heard, nor the human heart conceived, what God has prepared for those who love him," we read in 1 Corinthians 2:9 (NRSV). And *image* is the word to use here because what we can conjure up in our minds and hearts about God can only ever, at best, approximate his goodness and nearness, his pervasive and loving existence.

"We *are* his beloved children," Graves writes, "the apple of his eye. But sometimes we do not feel like beloved children. Especially in the barren lands of wilderness exhaustion, we can feel like abused and neglected children whose father failed to provide." The good news is that there is no need to talk ourselves into a cheerful attitude, to paste on smiles and platitudes about God's provision. We can and must be honest about our desert experiences. We can and must remain where we are called, listen for God's small, still voice, and remember the words of the psalmist, "I lift up my eyes to the hills. / From where will my help come? / My help comes from the LORD, / who made heaven and earth" (Ps. 121:1–2 ESV). God is the beauty without and within us, and it is God who lends the beauty to the disasters we create and inhabit. The beautiful disasters.

John Ortberg and Laura Ortberg Turner

this
wilderness
life

1

the way of the desert and beautiful souls

Do you want to be holy? Then you will suffer.

John Stott[1]

My Desert Wilderness Life

The phone rings. It is 9:27 on a frigid Thursday night in mid-February. I'm sitting in my cozy living room in my weekly meeting with the six college dorm resident assistants who work with me. The caller ID shows that it's my dad. I silence the phone. A little after ten o'clock, I begin listening to my messages. All three are from him. In the first, he almost incoherently tells me that my sister-in-law's sister just died of a heroin overdose, and before I am finished listening to the message, "Call Waiting" flashes on my phone screen. It's my dad again. He repeats his message: my sister-in-law's sister died of a heroin overdose. I thank him for letting me know and tell him that I plan on contacting my brother and his family immediately.

Suddenly I notice laughter and loud music in the background.

"Dad, where are you? Are you at a bar?"

"Yes," he says.

"Dad, are you drinking?"

"No, I am just drinking ice water."

"Dad, I don't believe you. I think you're lying. You know that you're not supposed to be drinking. You don't have to go to the bar to drink ice water."

"What's wrong with being at a bar? The church isn't against it. I'm allowed to dance and have some fun. I'm not going to listen to my daughter lecture me and call me a liar." Click.

The call resurrects the memories and now-faint emotions of an eight-year-old little girl. While my brother and sister slept peacefully, I'd fitfully lie awake, waiting up four, five, six or more hours for my dad to return from the bar or from God knows where. I'd lie in bed as stiff as a board, bracing myself for the worst possible outcome: his death due to drunk driving. I'd mentally and emotionally hold my breath until I heard him come in the door (my husband still catches me physically holding my breath every night and reminds me to breathe; I guess it has become ingrained). A good night's sleep and peace of mind depended on his safe return home. Needless to say, I slept little and had very little peace of mind.

I am not sure how it happened, but soon after the long period of staying up nights, my parents and I switched roles. By the time I was ten, I was a parent to my parents and to my younger sister and brother. Although I so desperately needed parenting, circumstances forced me to function as an adult in a child's body. Almost daily I tried to come up with adult-sized solutions to adult-sized problems.

I lived in a world of turmoil while supporting parents who were preoccupied trying to figure out their own lives and problems. Many days I felt as if my heart had been violently ripped out, thrown to the ground, stomped on, and left for scavengers. I became an emotional and spiritual orphan, left to figure things out and make my own messes. I was a child fending for myself in the wilderness. Since I had no one to turn to for guidance, I clung to verses in the book of Psalms that proclaimed God to be a Father to the fatherless. I begged him to father and mother me—to show me how to live. A song by Audioslave captures well my soul's sentiments at the time:

> Nail in my hand
> From my creator
> You gave me life
> Now show me how to live.[2]

You gave me life; now show me how to live. I needed God to show me his path through the desert wildernesses of poverty, DUIs, adultery, mental illness, prison, a house fire, the death of loved ones, poisonous relationships, and my own bad decisions. I needed him (and still need him) to show me how to live.

Even as I write these words, I am in a deep wilderness tied to the phone call I received from my dad that night in February. His drinking and carousing are driven by a severe bipolar condition and by his refusal to take medicine because he doesn't believe there is anything wrong with him. Because of my dad's behavior in the last six months, my parents are homeless, jobless, and penniless. They're destitute. And at this moment, my dad is in jail.

In this present wilderness, I pray, I write, and I depend on my brothers and sisters in the body of Christ to share my burdens. And I wait. I wait on God. The desert is so prevalent in my life that I've adopted it as the metaphor of my life. It seems that I

5

am in and out of the desert on a frequent basis. But I find that I am in good company.

Formation

Growing up, I begged God (what seems like thousands of times) to take the cup of suffering from me, but mostly he didn't. Instead, he used my pain and difficulties, my desert experiences, to transform me—which in turn alleviated much suffering. As I grew up in the desert, God grew my soul. And although I realize that the suffering I've endured is nothing compared to the suffering of countless millions, I've learned painful but essential lessons that I couldn't have learned anywhere else but in the midst of God-haunted suffering.

God uses the desert of the soul—our suffering and difficulties, our pain, our dark nights (call them what you will)—to form us, to make us beautiful souls. He redeems what we might deem our living hells, if we allow him. The hard truth, then, is this: everyone who follows Jesus is eventually called into the desert.

Jesus suffered hunger and temptation in the desert. His calling and his trust in his Father were put to the test. He was probably full of angst and despair. He was physically weak and emotionally and spiritually vulnerable. Why on earth would the Holy Spirit drive him into the desert wilderness and allow him to suffer?

Scripture is full of examples of how God used the desert to reveal himself and to spiritually form his people. Abraham, Hagar, Jacob, Miriam, Moses, the Israelites, David, Elijah, Jonah, John the Baptist, and Paul all spent time in the wilderness. They weren't alone either—the desert fathers and mothers made their homes in the wilderness too.

All these giants of the faith spent time in the physical desert but were also intimately acquainted with the interior desert.

Eventually, God sends all who truly seek to know him into a spiritual wilderness. That's why St. John of the Cross calls this dark night, this desert of ours, a "happy night." The night is happy because, though it brings "darkness to the spirit, it does so only to give it light in everything; . . . although it humbles it and makes it miserable, it does so only to exalt it and to raise it up."[3] N. T. Wright notes, "Wilderness has been used in Christian writing as an image for the dark side of the spiritual journey. Conversion, baptism, faith—a rich sense of the presence and love of God, of vocation and sonship; and then, the wilderness."[4] The spiritual desert wilderness is harsh, wild, and uncontrollable. Barely inhabitable and yet breathtakingly beautiful.[5] Inarguably dangerous and possibly deadly but also transformational and even miraculous. Solitary and unfamiliar but full of grace and spiritual activity.

The desert is a blessing disguised as a curse—a study in contrasts. While theophanies and divine epiphanies regularly occur there, so do unimaginable times of depression and despair. We hear many voices and sometimes have difficulty distinguishing among God's, our own, the world's, and that of devils toying with us, meaning to eat us alive. The desert heightens our senses; paradoxically, we're acutely aware of both God's presence and his seeming absence. Truths once obscure, or mentally assented to yet not experienced, suddenly stand out in sharp relief, while the superfluous recedes into the background. In the desert wilderness, miracles happen, temptations lure, and judgment occurs.

The wilderness has a way of curing our illusions about ourselves and teaching us to depend more and more on God.[6] When we first enter, we're convinced we've entered the bowels of hell. But on our pilgrimage, we discover that the desert drips with the divine. We discover that desert land is fertile ground for spiritual activity, transformation, and renewal. The desert mothers and

7

fathers knew this. Bradley Nassif, an Orthodox Christian and biblical scholar, tells us:

> The desert fathers and mothers heard Christ's call to deny themselves, take up their cross daily, and follow him (Luke 9:23) in a time similar to our own. Under Emperor Constantine, large numbers joined the church for the social privileges it bestowed. Many sought status and prosperity more than the cross. This influx of nominal Christians made the church a spiritually sick institution, and a radical illness called for a radical remedy. Ordinary men and women, most of them illiterate, heard the death-call of the gospel and responded by fleeing to the desert to live out their calling; either alone or in community. Peasants, shepherds, camel traders, former slaves, and prostitutes were the first to go.
>
> The desert was not a place of escape as much as a place of countercultural engagement. The desert was the front line of spiritual warfare; as in the Bible, a place of testing and death. It was where the heart was purified, the passions conquered, sin destroyed, and humanity renewed.[7]

Indeed, it's not just the solitude of the physical desert that works wonders in the soul. God uses our interior desert as a radical antidote to our spiritual sickness. It is the place where, with the prodigal, we come to our senses, the location where we realize God is more real than anything else.[8] It becomes a place of God-encounters, conversion, transformation, salvation, grace, renewal, redemption, and reconciliation. We learn to trust God in the wilderness, and then we die. But it is not our end, for there we are raised to new life—made fully alive, truly human.

Isaiah 35 describes the consummation of our wilderness experience: "The desert and the parched land will be glad; / the wilderness will rejoice and blossom. / Like the crocus, it will burst into bloom; / it will rejoice greatly and shout for joy" (vv.

1–2a). Our lives will not forever remain a barren wilderness. In our difficult experiences, we will see the glory of God as Isaiah says: "The glory of Lebanon will be given to it, / the splendor of Carmel and Sharon; / they will see the glory of the LORD, / the splendor of our God. . . . Water will gush forth in the wilderness / and streams in the desert" (vv. 2b, 6b). Our mourning will turn into gladness. "Gladness and joy will overtake them, / and sorrow and sighing will flee away" (v. 10). But while we're deep within the desert wilderness, we may not believe a word of what Isaiah tells us. Not a word.

The Purpose of the Desert Wilderness

According to theologian Robert Barry Leal:

> Especially in the Hebrew Bible, wilderness is the privileged site where God comforts the Hebrew people or their representatives at times of crisis in their lives. In the wilderness God calls and leads them to decisions and witnesses their shortcomings; and God disciplines and punishes them for their sin and rebellion. Throughout the gospels wilderness is important for Jesus as a place of encounter with the Father.[9]

As I mentioned earlier, I've been in and out of the desert wilderness my entire life. I've come to expect it. I've also realized that I'm not the only one who's been in and out of the wilderness; each of us, throughout our lives, journeys back and forth between wilderness and Promised Land. Just when we've gotten comfortable, we're plunged back in. And then in the blink of an eye, each of us moves from our final desert wilderness experience of death into the Promised Land of eternal life.

When I consider the desert experiences of others, I think of my husband's childhood friend Andy. He was a "wannabe" missionary turned police officer who, senselessly, was shot at point-blank range and killed when he intervened in a domestic violence dispute. It could've been anyone else, but he was the first officer on the scene. He was a seminary-trained, hardworking police officer for three reasons: he deeply cared about people and wanted to help them—to be Christ in uniform, he wanted to faithfully and adequately provide for his family, and he desired to earn money for his missionary voyage to Thailand. Yet, that was not to be. He died at the age of thirty, leaving behind a young wife, a five-year-old, a toddler, and an infant. Frankly, I don't know why God allowed him to suffer such a tragic, untimely death, nor do I wish to speculate and offer unsatisfying answers. All I can say is that somehow God wishes to meet his family and friends in the wilderness of loss and that God does not force anyone into the desert out of cruelty.

On the contrary, God's ultimate desire is to use our pain and suffering, our angst and desperation, what the ancients and others (including me) call desert experiences, to form us into Christ's image, to steel our relationship with him. The desert can become a place of intimacy with God, for he desires that we intimately know him and be intimately known by him. But how does God use these desert experiences (or dark nights of the soul) to form us—making us fully alive, one with him? In the following chapters, we'll explore in more detail just how he does that.

2

who am I?

It's haunting how I can't seem
To find myself again.
Linkin Park, "Crawling"

Whether consciously or subconsciously, many of us spend our time searching for our identities. Others of us are desperately seeking to shed them in favor of becoming someone else. "Who am I?" "Who can I become?" and "Where do I belong?" are the questions that claw at us, motivating much of our behavior. Upon reflection, we find that deep inside our souls dwells the haunting suspicion that who we are is a mere phantom of who we're meant to be. We're half alive, searching for life—searching for ourselves.

Amazingly, God often chooses to reveal who we are in the midst of suffering. This may come as a shock to us; after all, desert experiences are probably the last places we'd think to look in order to discover our God-given identities. Indeed, it seems incredibly strange that God would reveal our identities and his own in the crucible of pain. But he does.

God uses our identity crises to reveal who we are and who he is. Sometimes these crises come out of nowhere. Something devastating happens. Someone close to us dies. We are diagnosed, or someone we know is diagnosed, with a serious illness. Our families fall apart. We lose a job or don't get the job we're hoping for. We don't get into the school of our choice. A relationship goes downhill or never happens at all. We look into the mirror and realize we're old. We are thrown into painful disorientation. We start questioning everything. We're no longer sure of ourselves or of God. An internal crisis occurs.

All of us yearn for an identity, to know who we are at the core of our being, to be secure in who we are, and to be known for who we really are. We're tired of living in dysfunction. We long to be whole and healthy, to be the people God meant for us to be. Who can figure out who we are if we can't? This is an important question to consider, for wherever and to whomever you and I turn for answers will determine the quality of life we live.

For some of us, an identity crisis comes on suddenly, something triggers it. Others of us have been saddled with identity crises our entire lives. We've accepted identities that others foisted on us in their ignorance or exasperation or in the throes of their own suffering. These are names or identities we'd never choose for ourselves—names we can barely accept. We spend our lives trying to break free from and resisting the identities forced on us. They are like nooses around our necks, nooses that tighten the more we struggle.

Identity Changes

In Genesis 35, Jacob's wife Rachel names her son Ben-Oni just before she dies in childbirth. "Ben-Oni," roughly translated, means "son of my trouble" or "son of my pain." As little Ben-Oni learned to recognize his name, this tender and impressionable little one would blame himself for the death of his mother, a mother he never knew but deeply loved. With a name like Ben-Oni, he'd soon hemorrhage from the inside out. Just as it did with his mother, his lifeblood would slowly but surely trickle out of him.

That's why Jacob, his father, jumped into life-saving mode soon after his birth. He knew what was at stake. He immediately started CPR of the soul by renaming his newborn son. In renaming him Benjamin, Jacob gave him the gift of life—a fighting chance at a robust identity. In renaming him Benjamin, or "son of my right hand," Jacob was communicating that Benjamin was his precious, dear one, born to him in old age. Jacob was instilling a shalom-breathed identity into his son, saving him from years of shame and dysfunction.

Names are inseparable from identity, belonging, and place. Parents throughout the world hope that the names they give their children will describe their babies' personalities and roots. Their desire is for the name to shape that child's character and identity and, in the end, destiny. The hope is that a child will blossom into her name, into her calling.

Jacob himself was no stranger to name changes. Remember the story about him and his twin brother, Esau? Both had meaningful names—names that got at their identities. The name "Esau" is thought to mean "hairy."[1] Esau is also known as Edom, and "Edom" means "red." So in those days, when one heard the name Esau, one imagined the color red and lots of hair. "Oh, look!" they'd say. "Hairball is having a bad day. He's all red-faced because he's ticked off at his brother Jacob again." And, Esau had good reasons to be ticked off at Jacob.

"Jacob" means "he grasps the heel."[2] Figuratively, "Jacob" means "he deceives."[3] In those days, if Jacob appeared at the opening of your family tent hoping to sell you a few spotted lambs, you'd think, "What does full-of-deception Jacob want now? I don't know if he's telling the truth or pulling my leg. I don't know why I even do business with him." His name, "deceiver," makes you prone to think him a swindler even if he's one hundred percent honest in his sales pitch.

Throughout Jacob's story in Genesis, we see him scheming, even after he has a vision of God at Bethel. But God is merciful to Jacob, despite Jacob's seemingly undeserving, conniving ways. Remember Jacob's wilderness wrestling match with the angel of the Lord in Genesis 32? Jacob refused to forfeit the wrestling match. He refused to say "uncle"' until he received a blessing. However, Jacob's blessing was contingent on his admitting his name, or identity. The angel of the Lord asked, "What is your name?" and he answered, "Jacob" (deceiver).

The moment Jacob confessed his name—the moment he was brutally honest about himself, coming face-to-face with who he was and face-to-face with God—a supernatural transformation began. A theophany turned into an epiphany. In seeing God, Jacob saw himself for who he was. Seeing ourselves for who we are is always a miracle. Always. When Jacob confessed who he was instead of making excuses for himself and his behavior, God renamed him Israel. "Israel" means "he struggles with God" or "overcomer" or "let God rule." Jacob came to terms with himself and with God; therefore, the angel of the Lord gave him the most precious treasure of all: a new name that symbolized the blessing of his God-given identity and destiny.

God returned the man to himself, to who he was created to be. No longer was he Jacob the deceiver. That is, no longer could he deceive without a conscience. That would go against his nature. True, he had to grow into his name. He had to learn how to live into his redemption, to work out his salvation, his God-given identity, with fear and trembling. But there's no question about it—in renaming him, God set in motion an epic change in Jacob's heart. That moment, God began making all things new in Jacob's life and in the lives of his descendants. Jacob's God-given identity had eternal implications for himself and for others—for the entire earth.

That's how God operates when he changes someone's name. It is an outward symbol of an inward transformation and calling, of a new God-given identity and destiny. Pastor Edward F. Markquart puts it this way:

> His whole life he had been cheating, cheating, cheating. His whole life he had been manipulating people. His whole life he had been clever and cunning and that night, that night, in that wrestling match with God, God touched him. God touched him in such a way that he was changed. And God gave him a new name Israel, which means, let God rule. Any time in the Bible, when you get a new name, it is a sign of a dramatic and enormous change within that person.[4]

Markquart goes on to say, "And so Jacob underwent this enormous change from being Jacob to being Israel, from being a cheater and manipulator and cunning and clever to being a person who finally let God rule in his life."[5] Jacob woke up the next morning to a new life, and it was that morning that he was reconciled to his estranged twin brother, Esau. Every step Jacob took in this new life with his dislocated hip would be a reminder of his encounter with God, a reminder of his new name.

Becoming Twisted

Maybe in our desperate search for our identities we cloak ourselves with the derogatory labels given to us by mean-spirited or careless and clueless people. Interestingly enough, even seemingly "nice" Christian people deform us by carelessly tossing out names for us. Perhaps those closest to us are guilty of identity theft. And because we are vulnerable, tender shoots, we often grow into these clueless, careless estimations of ourselves instead of accepting God's Word to us and about us. Maybe we don't believe God thinks much of us anyhow. We feel abandoned by God. It's as though God gave birth to us but then left us for dead; he never showed us how to live. So we try to figure out life on our own.

Besides the fact that such feelings are not reflective of the reality of who God is, the problem is that not knowing God's estimation of us leaves us vulnerable to bullying and name-calling—to soul malformation because we have no standard by which to measure what is and isn't true. In his book *Jesus and the Disinherited*, Howard Thurman writes, "If a man knows precisely what he can do to you or what epithet he can hurl against you in order to make you lose your temper, your equilibrium, then he can always keep you under subjection. It is a man's reaction to things that determines their ability to exercise power over him."[6]

Epithets can chip away at the image of God in us. Name-calling and identity theft are felonious offenses against divinity and humanity. Blasphemy. Those of us who have been victims of identity theft or have been disfigured by name-calling dare not engage in such nefarious activity. We too will be blameworthy whether the offense is committed in our hearts, spoken with our mouths, or written with our hands.

This makes sense of why Jesus told his audience that anyone who labeled another person "*Raca*," or fool, was in danger of the fires of hell (Matt. 5:22). In the end, only God can identify a person's condition and make a righteous judgment. God knows our names and uses his beloved community to help form our God-given identities. But in our twisted state, in our malformation, we would rather choose our own names and also mistakenly

16

believe we can accurately name others. We strut about as if we are God.

Defamation

In high school, I made an almost fatal decision about my identity. I remember it well. It started when I tried out for the cheerleading squad at the end of my freshman year. To my great surprise, I made it. I had no desire to be a cheerleader per se. Frankly, I was thoroughly embarrassed by the little, short skirts we wore—especially during pep assemblies prior to big football games or wrestling matches. That's when we'd do kicks and stunts and moves, every angle of our bodies on display for the entire student body to see. I was extremely self-conscious about my body yet really wanted to socialize. My teenage search for identity and my desire to be intimately known and cared for led me to take name-making and life-making matters into my own hands. And so I entered a wilderness of my own making, a hellhole I had a hand in digging.

My sophomore year I began dating a wrestler who had the reputation of being a nice guy (though not a believer). One late afternoon about three weeks into the relationship, I felt the crushing conviction of the Holy Spirit. "Break up with him. You know you're not supposed to be doing this," the Spirit whispered. "Don't worry. I will soon." What a reversal—normally it's God or an angel telling God's people not to worry or fear. Yet somehow I felt the need to reassure God, to get him to relax. "Fear not, God," I said. I then proceeded to casually defy God because I thought I knew what was life-giving for me. I thought I'd have the fortitude to get rid of my boyfriend at will. I thought I'd obey in my own time. Obedience to God now meant that I'd miss out, or so I thought. I soon rued the day I disobeyed the Spirit's word to me.

17

The guy quickly shed his angel of light costume; he began to badger and tempt me to sink my teeth into the forbidden fruit. Through him I allowed sin to sink its teeth into me. It'd be a while before I could shake either him or my sin—and all for a split second of pleasure. What I was searching for was my name. I trusted him to tell me and reveal to me who I was. I thought our relationship would satisfy my thirst for identity and intimacy. But I discovered that he cared more about himself than me. More than once he forced himself on me. And more than once I asked him why he had done so. He actually said, "No means yes."

When he said that, you'd think I would've launched him out of my life, getting rid of him for good. But I had sold myself into emotional and physical slavery. It wasn't his sin alone. At times, I initiated. I too was at fault; I had become a slave to sin. I'd break up with him and then take him back when he came to me crying crocodile tears.

My family circumstances left me with a feverish soul that was permeated with pain. I thought a little sip of devil water would douse the fire-of-hell flames already licking at my soul. Instead, giving into him was like throwing gasoline on the fire. I incinerated myself.

Now I was sure that the hell fires would eventually consume my soul. Like Esau, I had sold my birthright for immediate gratification—a pot of stew. Like Judas, I'd hung around Jesus for a while and then betrayed him. It was over for me. The words of Hebrews 6:4–6 played over and over in my head, continually assaulting me:

> It is impossible for those who have once been enlightened, who have tasted the heavenly gift, who have shared in the Holy Spirit, who have tasted the goodness of the word of God and the powers of the coming age and who have fallen away, to be brought back

to repentance. To their loss they are crucifying the Son of God all over again and subjecting him to public disgrace.

I believed that I was, for all intents and purposes, damned. "Damned" was my name. It was my identity. Daily I cursed myself, punishing myself with these and other labels that I believed accurately identified me. It was as if I were straitjacketed in a car swerving down the road to perdition. I had lost control of my body and emotions. I saw no way out. Maybe that's how Judas felt after he betrayed Jesus. Maybe that's why he hanged himself—he saw no way to recover from his soul's disintegration. At the time, neither did I. I needed God to show me how to live, but I wasn't listening to him.

In our twisted and hurting states, in our search for ourselves, for our identities, we often butcher our own names because we've accepted what others or our environment says about us. As a result, we assume aliases that deform us. Our aliases morph into pigeonholes we can't crawl out of, labels we can't escape—self-fulfilling prophecies. We do things we'd never imagine doing when we are in our right minds—as I did.

My identity was intertwined with this guy. I didn't believe I had a life or could have a life apart from him. I had degenerated. I was looking up from rock bottom, thinking I was fated to continue this godforsaken lifestyle. I felt doomed to right my wrongs by marrying him at seventeen or eighteen years of age.

But I couldn't. As I called out to God all day long and ruminated on Scripture, particularly verses in Isaiah and Jeremiah, hope crystallized within. As hope planted itself within me, I started believing that maybe, just maybe, Jesus wouldn't kick me when I was down. Maybe there was hope for me, and maybe Jesus had a new name for me. Verses such as Isaiah 42:3 and Jeremiah 3:12–14 resuscitated me.

> He will not crush the weakest reed
> or put out a flickering candle.
> He will bring justice to all who have been wronged.
> (Isa. 42:3 NLT)

> "'Return, faithless Israel,' declares the LORD,
> 'I will frown on you no longer,
> for I am faithful,' declares the LORD,
> 'I will not be angry forever.
> Only acknowledge your guilt—
> you have rebelled against the LORD your God,
> you have scattered your favors to foreign gods
> under every spreading tree,
> and have not obeyed me,'"
> declares the LORD.
> "Return, faithless people," declares the LORD, "for I am your
> husband." (Jer. 3:12–14)

So, for the hundredth time, I resolved to break up with him and flee his presence for good. God heard the cries of my fractured soul, and like the Good Samaritan, Jesus had mercy on me.

Revelation of Our Identities

Before God can divulge our God-given identities in our desert-of-the soul wilderness experiences, there is something we need to know: he requires that we be brutally honest with ourselves and with him—just as Jacob was. If we desire to find out who we are, we have to confess who we have been. What is our name? Who are we right now? That is, what defines us, what condition are we in, what has been our bent? Are we lust-filled, greedy, or self-righteous? Are we blind to our own sin, deceptive, full of pride, or adulterous? Do we exhibit laziness, a weak will, or fear? Are we manipulators and opportunists, materialistic or addicted? Are we living independently of God? It seems that I've been most of those at one time or another. Thomas Merton reminds us that "we are not very good at recognizing illusions, least of all the ones we cherish about ourselves."⁷ Yet God is keenly aware of our tendency to cherish self-illusions. Being confronted by a friend, confessing my sins to her and to God, praying, recognizing this guy's sorry ways, and reading verses in Jeremiah 2 and 3 helped me come face-to-face with who I was. I learned and confessed my without-God names. "She-camel" was one of the false names I had to confess. These verses from Jeremiah tell the story of who I felt I was at that time:

> "I remember the devotion of your youth,
>   how as a bride you loved me
> and followed me through the wilderness,
>   through a land not sown.
>   . . . .
> I brought you into a fertile land
>   to eat its fruit and rich produce.
> But you came and defiled my land
>   and made my inheritance detestable.
>   . . . .
> Consider then and realize
>   how evil and bitter it is for you
> when you forsake the LORD your God.
>   . . . .
> See how you have behaved in the valley;
>   consider what you have done.
> You are a swift she-camel
>   running here and there,
> a wild donkey accustomed to the desert,
>   sniffing the wind in her craving—
>   in her heat who can restrain her?

. . . .

Look up to the barren heights and see.
Is there any place where you have not been ravished?"
(2:2, 7, 19, 23–24; 3:2)

There was no doubt that I was guilty of the sins mentioned in these verses. These sins were deep within me. How could I deny them? All I can say is, "Thanks be to God!" Instead of cringing and scampering out of the light and into dark recesses like a cockroach, I stood there naked under the laser beam of God's holiness.

Not only do we have to confess our unholy names (sins and unholy bents and dispositions) to God, but we also need to confess our false names and identities to trusted others within the beloved community for transformation to happen. As James 5:16 tells us, healing happens when we come clean with one another and pray for one another.

We will have to be prepared for what happens when we do come face-to-face with God and ourselves in the desert wilderness and then choose to confess what we see. One look at ourselves in the divine mirror and we're horrified—horrified because for the first time we realize our true condition. We discover that we're guilty of hideous, deeply ingrained sins we were too self-righteous to see before, sins we quickly identified in others but were blind to in ourselves. And even when we recognize our sins, we find that we more readily excuse in ourselves what we despise in others. That is, we cut ourselves the slack we refuse to cut others.

It is only in coming face-to-face with God and our self-illusions that we are ultimately stripped of those illusions and false identities. That is purification. It doesn't happen in an instant but little by little throughout our lives as our hearts are transformed to look like Jesus's heart. If God were to instantaneously transform us into who he created us to be, to at once right all the wrong in us, to at once purify us of everything in us that is not of him, that would be the death of us. Don't we writhe in pain when he begins to peel off layers of falsehood like one would peel off a Band-Aid? It's a painful process, one I believe is best depicted in C. S. Lewis's *Voyage of the Dawn Treader* when Eustace is undragoned.

Acknowledging our profound depravity and receiving God's forgiveness will drive us to profound gratitude and humility—because we are scandalized by his goodness, beauty, and grace. And it's in that posture that the process of purifying us from our unholy labels begins. In our posture of gratitude and humility, the Lord breathes new life into us. Each time we shed a false name or label, that part of us becomes a new creation of beauty. This happens throughout our lives, and that's how, little by little, we become beautiful souls.

And the wonderful thing is that when God reconciles all things to himself, when he is finished purifying us, when he is finished remaking us into Christ's image, he'll reveal the full meaning and implications of our names. Revelation 2:17 tells us, "Whoever has ears, let them hear what the Spirit says to the churches. To the one who is victorious, I will give some of the hidden manna. I will also give that person a white stone with a new name written on it, known only to the one who receives it."

On that day, God and each one of us will be the only ones who have a full understanding of our God-given identities. On that day, when we receive our new names, we will throw our heads back, our jaws will drop, and our bodies will convulse with the heartiest and most joyous of belly laughter because reality will turn out to be better than anything we could've asked for or imagined. We'll finally know full intimacy and who we are. God will gift us with the names we've been searching for our entire lives.

God's Name

Interestingly enough, not only does God reveal our true identities in the desert, but he also reveals his own identity, for he desires that we know him intimately on this earth. God's name reveals his character and purpose. His very being and our own welfare are wrapped up in his name, his identity.

On this earth, then, in our deserts, God personally reveals and names himself. When he does so, his pleasure floods our senses, his beauty engulfs us, and our God-misconceptions are devastated. He moves us from make-believe to reality. The knowledge of who he is and the never-ending implications of being his children overwhelm us.

Remember that it was while he was in the desert that Moses learned God's great name, "I AM" (Exod. 3:14). And it was in the desert that God showed Moses his glory by declaring his name: "The LORD, the LORD, the compassionate and gracious God, slow to anger, abounding in love and faithfulness, maintaining love to thousands, and forgiving wickedness, rebellion and sin" (Exod. 34:6–7).

God's glory is in his name. And so our lostness and disorientation in life, our not knowing our names, ultimately come from not knowing God intimately. If we don't know God, it's impossible to really know ourselves and our place in the redemption story. In *The Divine Conspiracy*, Dallas Willard writes, "It is a great and important task to come to terms with what we really think when we think of God. Most hindrances to the faith of Christ, actually lie, I believe, in this part of our minds and souls."[8]

God uses the wilderness experiences in our lives to teach us his name. If we, like Moses, wish to see God's glory, it will often be in the wilderness that we see it. The beauty of the desert experience is in beholding God. It's as if he woos us out into the wilderness so we can behold him. In the desert, he seeks to know us and to be known by us. As we behold him, we come to know him. We learn his name and his ways and become increasingly whole. To borrow a phrase from Father Greg Boyle, "We marinate in the intimacy of God."⁹

Throughout our wilderness experiences, we will become familiar with different facets of God's character and thus different aspects of his name. There are a variety of circumstances in which we will come to know God intimately as *Jehovah Jireh*—"God our provider"—not just a financial provider but the provider of our wholeness and the wholeness of others. In our injury and in our sicknesses, we will come to him, needing him to be the "God who heals us," *Jehovah Rapha*. He is Jehovah Rapha for us and also for the world. God will nurture deep trust in us as we begin to discover who he is as revealed in his names throughout Scripture. In our desert experiences, probably more so than at any other time, we learn just who God is and, consequently, who we are.

It is good to remember that when we enter a new wilderness experience, it is easy to forget who we are. And when we forget who we are and whose we are, circumstances go downhill quickly. Feasting on the wisdom of the desert fathers and mothers and of the Orthodox tradition, John Chryssavgis tells us, "Unfortunately, the reality is that we tolerate being less than we are called to be. Pride is not the ultimate sin; forgetfulness of our origin and destiny is, in fact, the ultimate tragedy."¹⁰

After my wilderness experience in high school, God changed my names from "Impure She-camel," "Adult in Child-sized Body," and "Depressed" to "Pure in Heart," "Child," and "Fully Alive in the Kingdom of God." My past actions no longer defined me. My identity was wrapped up in God and his actions and his story. God gave me new life and new definition to my life. He bestowed on me the blessing of a God-given identity. I was free to figure out who I was and to whom I belonged. For the first time, I was learning how to live.

These days, I am sure to practice the discipline of remembering who I am and the discipline of living accordingly because I remember what happens when I don't.

3

to your cell
for goodness's sake

> But silence speaks of solitude, and to some persons there is an
> oppressive sense of sadness wherever human beings are absent.
> Solitude is so awful to them. . . . Some men flee to solitude
> through bitterness of spirit, through hatred of the world, be-
> cause of disappointment, blight, or sorrow. Others go because
> in the vastness of the desert the spirit finds freedom and en-
> largement, and hence, peace.
>
> George Wharton James

My painful childhood experiences drove me to immerse myself
in Scripture. In fifth through seventh grades, after my chores, I'd
often cloister myself in my closet of a room in our flimsy-walled,
green trailer in the hills of Northwest Pennsylvania for up to
three hours a day to read the Bible. The other alternative was
to fritter away my time watching television. But since I usually
found television uninteresting, I opted for my room.

My life was a wilderness of pain that created in me an insatiable hunger for God. I also had an insatiable desire for intimacy with God. In the trailer, I read with my back against the wall, sitting on my unadorned mattress and box spring, the only piece of furniture we managed to squeeze into the room. The scant light from the window slit (installed too high up for me to see through) combined with the dangling, low-watt ceiling light bulb, in dire need of a light fixture, made for dimly lit reading. There was no place for a lamp even if I wanted one. And if there were room for one, a new lamp was a luxury we couldn't afford. Back then, there were no Goodwill stores close by.

I had no toys to speak of. My only possessions consisted of a few outfits, a small radio I plugged in and set down on the narrow footpath between the bed and the opposite wall, and my black, leather-bound, large-print King James Bible. The Bible was a Christmas gift from my parents in fifth grade.

My room was rather depressing, really. Devoid of beauty. When I was tired, I'd lie on my side with my head on the pillow, prop my Bible on the bed, and continue to soak in visions of God that had come to life. I was like Jacob at Bethel with visions of angels ascending and descending on the ladder to heaven. (Except that he was outside with a stone for a pillow.)

I spent the majority of my time in the Old Testament. There, I'd trail a few feet behind, observing as Adam and Eve walked and talked with the Lord in Eden at dusk. I very much wished to enter into the conversation. I became jealous of them. Adam and Eve had God's undivided attention. I wanted to have that sort of intimacy with him. I wanted God's attention all to myself—his undivided attention.

In those days, whenever anyone asked me my favorite verse, I'd cite Genesis 5:24 from my King James Bible: "And Enoch walked with God: and he was not; for God took him." If I could just grow close enough to God, I believed, walking and talking with him every chance I had, then maybe I too would be translated up to heaven like Enoch or Elijah. People would look for me, but like the two holy men, I would've vanished into thin air. I didn't see any reason it couldn't be so.

If I lingered long enough, I assumed I had a good chance of seeing God or some angel or even the Virgin Mary. I had heard stories of the Virgin Mary and angels appearing to children in other countries. Once, when I was eleven, on a warm sunny day in the middle of the summer, I took my brother and sister out into a field to wait on God. I thought I'd try my hand at becoming a recipient of these appearances. I remember draping a blanket about my shoulders like a cape. What for, I can't remember. The three of us stood in the field, locked arm in arm, blinking in the sunshine. We waited and we waited. Nothing happened, nothing at all. It could've been ten minutes, but to young me it seemed like twelve hours. The adventure turned out to be an epic disappointment. I figured that for reasons known only to him, God deemed me unworthy of divine appearances, no matter how hard I mustered my willpower to wish them into reality. Neither God nor the Virgin Mary nor his angel Gabriel appeared—no matter how hard I prayed. My little brother and sister were unphased. We turned around. I trudged back inside the trailer and returned to the Scriptures.

I trembled with the Israelites as they stood in fright, looking at the Egyptian army with the sea at their backs. I triumphantly crossed the Red Sea with the grand caravan, looking up, marveling at the great ocean walls towering above. Every now and then I'd plunge my right hand into the seawater wall and accidently spray salt water onto my face.

I morphed into Caleb or Joshua, the only two spies to make it to the Promised Land. I was furious that the others didn't believe God would make good on his promise to give us the land. I watched Samson bring down the house on himself and

29

his tormentors. I admired and identified with Deborah, the prophetess, priestess, and national leader. And I heard God affectionately speak to me the words he spoke about Israel and Ephraim, the objects of his affection in Hosea 11:3–4. "It was I who taught Ephraim to walk, taking them by the arms. . . . / I led them with cords of human kindness, / with ties of love. / To them I was like one who lifts / a little child to the cheek, / and I bent down to feed them." God was holding me, a scared little girl, and lifting me up to his cheek. Thus, I entered the scriptural narrative, and the narrative entered me.

Just a few years ago, I discovered that the way I naturally read Scripture has a name: *lectio divina*. Only when I became older did I realize that I would've died in the wilderness because of my disobedience, and that I too have played the part of Judas in the life of Jesus. In my young naïveté, I always pictured myself as the obedient and faithful one in the Bible stories. Now, not so much.

When I wasn't reading inside, I'd spend hours cutting and stacking wood with my younger brother and sister so our family could earn extra income. Although I lived a sheltered existence as a child, I benefited from a life full of solitude and silence and excursions into nature, where I encountered the powerful beauty, glory, and goodness of God. We had fields and streams and woods all around us. While I wasn't so much sheltered by my parents, I was sheltered by the isolated geography and poverty that hemmed me in and that God ultimately used to incubate my soul.

Within me grew the divine imagination. As I ruminated on the words of God, they implanted deep within me. And so early on I learned I must apply what I read. The first agonizing application I made was a result of reading the words in Matthew 6:14–15: "For if you forgive other people when they sin against you, your heavenly Father will also forgive you. But if you do not forgive others their sins, your Father will not forgive your sins." These were hard words to swallow as an eleven-year-old.

A year or so before I read these verses, we lived in Levitown, Puerto Rico. One day I stepped off my school bus along with my brother and sister and a group of other children. A man drove up to us, rolled down his window, and beckoned me over. In Spanish, he asked me if I knew the directions to Palo Alto. Even back then I wanted to be helpful, though I didn't know how to get to Palo Alto. As I walked over to his window, I saw he sat exposed. He grabbed my hand and tried to force me to touch his genitals. I screamed in horror. I still remember his face, his sinister grin of pleasure at my expense. The rest of the kids were trudging along a couple of hundred feet away. They had no idea what was happening. I didn't tell them what happened because I was embarrassed and thought it was my fault, but I did tell my mom and *abuelita* when I got home. It was there by the bus stop that I lost my innocence. I couldn't get his perverted grin and the rest of him out of my head. The picture lodged itself in my memory. I'm reminded of this warning of Jesus's: "If anyone causes one of these little ones—those who believe in me—to stumble, it would be better for them if a large millstone were hung around their neck and they were thrown into the sea" (Mark 9:42).

After what happened, I feared being in the presence of grown men. Even a year later, when I was in the grocery store with my mother, I couldn't enter any checkout line that had a male cashier. I felt dirty. But when I read those words in Matthew 6:14–15, I knew I had to forgive this man, this man whose name I never knew but whose face I'd never forget, even if he forgot mine. I had to forgive him if I wanted God to forgive me. So at eleven years of age, I chose to forgive him.

And so my little closet room in the green trailer served as my first monastic cell. There I learned that God cared for me, delivered me, and conversed with me as he did with those in Scripture. There I learned I had to forgive others if I wanted God to forgive me. In my cell, supposed theological sophistication hadn't yet taught me to qualify what God could and couldn't do. It is where I grew up in God. There is a story told about the fourth-century desert father, Abba Moses. A brother went to Moses to ask for advice. He said to him, "Go and sit in your cell, and your cell will teach you everything."[1] Indeed, it has.

Solitude Births Souls of Renown

Jochebed, the mother of the biblical Moses, broke the law by refusing to obey Pharaoh's decree mandating that all male Hebrew infants be drowned in the river. She would not drown her son or let anyone else drown him. She would not! Instead, she sent him sailing down the Nile in a little basket boat. How many other babies had been drowned in the Nile? How many Hebrew families had to witness the horror of having their baby boys thrown in the river or live with the guilt of drowning their precious ones? Jochebed took the calculated risk of pushing the little boat out into the river, close to the Egyptian princess's regular bath time, so that the princess might notice the baby and take pity on him. Quite providentially, her plan worked.

Moses's basket was trapped among the reeds, and his high-pitched shrieks shattered the death-filled silences of the Nile, drawing attention to his helplessness. The unnamed Egyptian princess heard his cries and had compassion on him. Immediately, she commanded her servants to fetch him from the reeds, thereby rescuing him from certain death. Then the rest of Jochebed's plan unfolded. Moses's sister, Miriam, had planted herself close to the princess's entourage so that she could offer the wet nurse services of her mother. In the kind of twist that God's divine story lines are known for, the Egyptian princess provided for Moses while Jochebed nursed him. Somewhere along the way, probably through Jochebed or Miriam, Moses learned about the God of his ancestors. God had blessed Egypt through their ancestor Joseph in a time of famine, and the God of Abraham had promised to bless the entire earth through his people, the Hebrews.

The thought of Hebrew blood pumping through his veins, along with the recognition that his grandfather Pharaoh was the source of his people's misery, tormented Moses. When he finally understood how things worked, the way of his Egyptian world, compassion and rage filled his heart. He could no longer ignore the plight of his people. He could no longer participate in and benefit from his grandfather's evil regime with a clean conscience. Egypt had raised him. Yet in her inhumane treatment of the Hebrews, Egypt was quickly becoming the enemy. He was torn.

He'd never forget the day he killed the Egyptian overseer. Never. Anger had gotten the best of him. The instant he witnessed the overseer beating his fellow Hebrew, he realized he'd have none of it. He lunged at the overseer, and fell upon him, striking him with blow after vicious blow. Moses was intent on making sure that the overseer paid for every last bit of pain he had inflicted on so many others. In his blind rage, Moses pummeled him.

When he came to his senses, the overseer's frozen face and lifeless body were stark evidence of a wild fury. Full-blown sin. When he stared into the dead man's face, Moses couldn't shake the feeling that he was staring straight at himself. That frozen face mirrored the condition of his deadened soul and forced him to realize just how thoroughly he had submitted to Egypt's evil spell. Sure, it had been a moment of passion, of murderous rage. Maybe he hadn't intended to kill the overseer. No matter. He had allowed Egypt's darkness to kill him. Thus, killing begat killing. (I wonder if this is part of the reason Moses was inspired to allow for cities of refuge. Moses understood the need for refuge.)

Moses had morphed into what he despised and was now guilty of using Egypt's murderous ways to solve problems. And he was sorry, so sorry. Hurriedly, he buried the body in a shallow grave. He couldn't bear to look at that face any longer. He had to put the whole thing behind him. His concern now was to make sure he wasn't found out. He'd do his best to make sure it didn't happen again. He couldn't let it happen again. Yet, unbeknownst to him at the time, someone had seen what he had done—another Hebrew. Moses's sin found him out. Years later, Moses understood that there was no way he could've run away from himself or what he had done. He couldn't escape reality.

As he sat in the desert tending sheep, the silences of Sinai suffocated his shrieks of desperation as he wound his way down memory lane. He couldn't help but recall his life as a prince and what it was like to hold court in Pharaoh's palace. He relished being held in high esteem. Those memories were such a contrast to the present. Back then he was somebody, an Egyptian prince for goodness sake. Now he was forgotten, a godforsaken, lonely shepherd banished from civilization.

I wonder if Moses had any inkling of God's plans for his life prior to the murder. I imagine his family must've pleaded with him, as a member of Pharaoh's household and an Egyptian prince, to do what he could to alleviate his people's suffering. After all, he was perfectly situated to somehow intervene on their behalf. Perhaps the idea that he would play a part in delivering his people from evil motivated his actions on that fateful day, the murderous day that forever changed his life.

Moses replayed the murder scene over and over in his head year after year. If only he hadn't killed the overseer. If only he had ignored the overseer's actions, he wouldn't be in this damnable place. Here he sat in a desert regretting all he had done and, in some ways, who he had become. Could his sins be forgiven, washed away in a land with little water? Was there any hope left for him? After years of thinking about it, he decided that he must've been delusional in thinking that the God of his ancestors had special plans for him. He was no deliverer. His youthfulness fled the day he fled Egypt. He was a weathered old man who could never go home again. A has-been. All he had were memories, and even those were starting to fade.

Purification and Redemption

Numbers 12:3 says that Moses, the leader of renown who is of no small import in the world's three major religions, was more humble than anyone else on earth. Despite having a wife, children, and extended family, he spent vast expanses of time alone, tending sheep. His humility, his strength, his intimacy with God and utter dependence on God were forged in the obscurity of desert silences, not in the thick of things. Moses would not have been Moses, the most humble man on earth, had he not spent eighty of his 120 years in the wilderness. He spent an entire lifetime there. His was a soul formed in the barren desert.

Before he trod on holy ground, he experienced years of alienation from himself, his family of origin, and his culture. His self-confidence? Down the drain. He'd left Egypt in his prime, at age forty. Now he had fallen to pieces. He couldn't even talk right; he felt helpless and useless. Discouraged. All the king's horses and all the king's men couldn't put him back together again, or so he thought. Moses didn't know who he was anymore. He only knew who he had been.

God used those forty years prior to the burning bush theophany to purify Moses of the Egypt within and to form in him life, the God-life. It was impossible for Moses to fathom just how enslaved he was to the Egyptian ways of being and doing. In Egypt, he was in charge; servants were at his beck and call. He had full authority. In the desert, he had no authority except over the sheep, his only subjects.

In Egypt, Moses was the master though enslaved. In the desert, he learned servitude, freely becoming Yahweh's obedient slave. God used Moses's suffering in the obscurity of desert silences to strip him of independence. God taught Moses obedience through what Moses suffered (Heb. 11:24–25). In the desert, he had to learn that he must always obey God and not his own inclinations. Otherwise he would die. The Lord knew that before Moses could deliver others, he needed to be delivered first—thus the desert.

As Moses's circumstances pushed him into the submissive posture of having to entrust himself to God, he became acutely aware that his Father in heaven, his Lord, was trustworthy. Silence taught him to distinguish God's voice from the cacophony of voices within and without. And so, little by little, he was purified and, subsequently, transformed.

Moses's purification enabled him to see God. As Jesus tells us, it is the pure in heart who see God (Matt. 5:8). I don't believe Moses was capable of seeing the burning bush as a new desert refugee. As we become adept at spotting God in the desert, it grows easier for us to spot him in the everyday. It was in the desert that Moses of Egypt was delivered. It was there that he became Moses, the most humble man on earth.

A Chosen Silence

There is a silence we choose. Our retreats into our cells of silence and solitude still the noise pollution in our lives so that we might eventually be still. Quieted enough to hear the whispers of God. Still enough to feel the Holy Spirit winds blowing through our lives and to observe the effects of the Spirit winds all around us. We retreat in hopes of delight, in hopes of tasting the good, the true, and the beautiful, which remind us of our Lord, whom we adore. We won't be disappointed. When we routinely immerse ourselves in life-giving quiet that we might sense the presence and guidance of God, he comes and makes his home with us. But we must be still, resting in a posture of openness to whatever comes—without expectation.

In the sometimes dark silence and stillness, our eyes adjust. We acquire night vision so that even on the darkest of nights we're eventually able to see the glory and faithfulness of God. In the dark, silent night, we're able to clearly see the beautiful truths concealed by the helter-skelter of a too-busy, disintegrated daily life. The truths have been there all along.

As with Moses, our hidden life—how we live in obscurity—is what shapes our character. In this intentional pilgrimage into the desert, our battered, bruised, and banged-around selves can finally crawl out of the fetal position. This is a space where we stretch out to reinvigorate the parts of us that have atrophied. It's where the stress fractures of our lives heal. The silent solitary space is where we journey to convalesce. Here we gain our footing and strength. Here we can finally breathe freely while silently seeking understanding. This cell is simultaneously a hospital for the soul and a training ground for holiness.

Our intentional pilgrimage is not only a form of self-care but also a form of communal care. It demonstrates our deep concern for others. If we truly love others or seek to love others, we'll detach ourselves from them for a while, trusting that our time alone with God will sensitize us to their needs and concerns. Here God teaches us how to treat others. Solitary experiences with God form in us the kind of character that loathes sinning against another. Therein we find the motivation to do good to others, and we learn how to do good to others too, including our enemies. Through the lens of silence, we see others more clearly and thus do justice instead of violence to who they are. As a result, our capacity for hospitality is increased, and we become better able to love others well. Solitude is a refuge where individual and, consequently, communal well-being is restored.

As we practice this discipline of detachment, God reassures us of his love for us. Dwelling in our cell for a good period of time prevents us from routinely falling apart while trying to live our basic, everyday lives. Without solitude, we cannot fathom just how enslaved we are. So many of us are chained to the opinions of others. We're addicted to praise and affirmation and eviscerated by criticism. Vainly, we busy ourselves (as Dallas Willard and Jan Johnson say) in managing the impressions others have of us. We exhaust ourselves in trying to become somebody in their eyes. In an interview with reporters, Pope Francis I offered this insight regarding the hidden life and obscurity of the Vatican administration: "There are saints among the Roman Curia. . . . As always, the ones who aren't saints make the most noise. . . . A single tree falling makes a sound, but a whole forest growing doesn't."[2] Saints are intentional about living a quiet, hidden life. They are not involved in noisy efforts to draw attention to themselves.

We simply cannot live our whole lives in full view of others—in the crowd. Our lives are not a peep show. Without the discipline of silence and solitude, we play to the crowds, always performing yet never being quite sure of ourselves. We become puppets on a string, easily manipulated by circumstances and the flimsy whims of others. Silence and solitude leech these poisonous addictions out of us. In the silent and solitary place, we hunker down in obscurity. It's just us and God. We don't have to impress anyone. We are who we are. Naked. Our vulnerabilities exposed. This silent space affords us the opportunity to take a good, hard look at ourselves. As with Moses, in this space, we are freed from external distractions. We force ourselves to forego the pursuit of seeking affirmation from others. Eventually, our internal unrest is stilled, and we are freed from the opinion of others.

A Modern-Day Escape to the Solitary Desert

Our solitary place is where we pay attention to our lives (as Frederick Buechner implores us to do).[3] Reflecting on our lives in this grand silence is like sitting in the front row of an amphitheater and watching the comedy and tragedy of our lives play out before us. Decisions about what we must renounce and what we must cling to come to the fore. A pilgrimage into silence and solitude with God enables us to take a step back so that we can filter reality from unreality and get our priorities straight. Within this stillness we find rest for our exhausted souls. If we want to learn how to live our ordinary lives well, we must regularly make a pilgrimage into solitude and silence so that we might consider our lives.

Bidding adieu to the internet and social media is a contemporary way of fleeing to the desert. While the internet is a convenient way to keep in touch with family and friends and to plumb the depths of knowledge, it is also a means of indulging our idle curiosities and nearly insatiable appetites for attention, affirmation, fame, and influence. These means tempt me to exchange intimacy with God and my family for the intimacies of a screen. They tempt me to run my life aground for an adulterous relationship.

The internet and social media feed my inordinate cravings for recognition. I think of the words C. S. Lewis penned in his preface to *Paradise Lost*: "In the midst of a world of light and love, of song and feast and dance, [Lucifer] could find nothing to think of more interesting than his own prestige."[4] Dare I choose

39

pursuit of prestige over loving and being present to those closest to me? Is my own prestige so important that I'd choose virtual engagement over incarnational living, over enjoying the good gifts God has given me apart from the screen? Fear of being left out or left behind is another reason it is difficult to pry myself away from the strong allure of social media. I fear being left out of the goings-ons of my friends or acquaintances I admire.

Given these propensities, I find that I am like Eustace in C. S. Lewis's *Voyage of the Dawn Treader*, who when "sleeping on a dragon's hoard with greedy, dragonish thoughts in his heart . . . had become a dragon himself."[5] A glimpse of myself in this state and I am horrified. For I see myself. I've become a dragon and need Christ to "undragon" me. I wrestle with the desire of wanting to hurl my computer out the window just to be done with the matter. But going to extremes is easier than the discipline of moderation. Going to extremes is simpler than living in a nuanced reality, the way reality in fact is.

So in the last three years, in order to reorient myself and head back onto the narrow way, I've given up social media and/or the internet for Lent. At first it's agonizing. I'm like a caffeine or nicotine addict going through withdrawal. I get all panicky and shaky, wondering what to do with myself. My fears assail me with the tales of all the fun, banter, and insider information I am missing. I'm nearly asphyxiated by the thought that I am left behind or uninvited, that I am an outsider looking in while others are living the good, glamorous life of connectedness. I fight the urge to check in. As Lent carries on, my urge slowly subsides. To some extent, I experience my life as it was before the internet. I read more books. I am more fully present to my family and friends. I hear God better. I am less hurried, more like God, who is never in a hurry. In Lenten silence and solitude via social-media fasts, I discover the words of Isaiah 30:15 to be true: "In repentance and rest is your salvation, / in quietness and trust is your strength." It is a soul-soothing time.

I realize that I need to flee to this desert more frequently. Probably, weekly. My Lenten practice has become a regular spiritual discipline. It allows me to disentangle myself from the cares of the world and follow Jesus more closely. It allows me to better love others.

Let All Mortal Flesh Keep Silence

There are different forms of silence, such as the silence of pain. There are caverns of pain and ends of worlds where what is too horrible to mention leaves us speechless. In these moments, we must allow the silent stillness to do its work. We cannot force speech just to fill the empty void. We must allow God to do his work within this solitary space in his time. It really is best that we don't speak. In these moments, let me be, and I'll let you be.

These are Job times—times when we are too numb for company. Speaking and listening wear us out. Words, even from the well-meaning, inflict wounds. And so we are forced to embrace the silence with all its healing and restorative qualities. We can't rush silence. It's a holy place. It's the space where God appears and where he works to purify and fortify our souls.

Silence is refreshing and liberating when, through it, God fills us to overflowing—after the cares of this world have worn us down, draining the life right out of us. In silence, God comes to us and purges us of poison.

We must also keep silence if we are to live and speak responsibly. Otherwise, we pollute the earth with our lives and with our speech. This is perhaps one explanation for why there is so much irresponsible Christian living and Christian-speak. Shallow people have not kept silence. A barrage of words, constant noise, internal and external, is akin to soul torture. For us to refuse silence and solitude means we embrace anemic Christianity. And anemic Christianity isn't Christianity at all. At best, it's Christianity on life support. Even Socrates knew that the unexamined life is not worth living.

I think one reason God stopped speaking on the seventh day, one reason he rested, is that he wanted to revel in the beauty and goodness of his creation. Resting and reveling in silent solitude—at play in the fields of the Lord—is divine recreation.

The Oppressive Silence of God?

And yet, silence can be brutally oppressive when we desperately strain to hear a word from God but do not. What happens to us when we experience long and expansive silences combined with solitude that leave us despairing, empty, and numb? What of God's silence?

We may wonder, "God, why are you silent in the face of the millions of atrocities against the innocent? Why on earth are you silent?"

But maybe his is a silence that speaks most loudly. Maybe he is so ravaged by the horrors that some of his children commit that he keeps silent. It may be that atrocities too horrible to mention render him speechless. He has no words for the unspeakable. His silence is not indicative of his refusal to bring forth justice or to right all wrongs. Perhaps his silence is his way of taking it all in—taking in the screams, the agonies, the horrors of the innocent, those whose voices are cut off before their time, never to be heard again. None of the evil is lost on him. And so he is silent. Let us not confuse God's silence with apathy. We want to goad God into speaking before it is time. This he does not do. This he will not do. God will not be hurried in his grief. Our God is a God who gives grief its time. He laments fully.

When God is silent, we might feel as though he has abandoned us just when we need him most. It's as if a parent or spouse who is supposed to care deeply for us has abandoned us. This seemingly cruel silence can haunt us like a house that was once full of the laughter, banter, and everyday rigmarole of friends, family members, children, or spouses who are no more.

And so we all have, or will have, those moments when we cry with Jesus, "My God, my God, why have you forsaken me?" Moments of anguish met with silence. Silence because we receive no explanation, or satisfactory explanation, for the end of our worlds. What makes these moments even more brutal is that we have no evidence that things will get better. We have no hope that we will see God's goodness in the land of the living. We have no hope that there is indeed a hope and a future for us. Even those closest to us prove to be of no comfort.

In the garden of Eden, it was God who went looking for Adam and Eve when they wandered off to hide in their shame. As he searched for them, he called out, "Where are you?" But in our dark desert silence, roles are reversed. It is we who search for God, weakly calling out, "God, where are you?" In these moments, it's as if God is the one who has gone AWOL, wandered off, or fallen asleep. God is the one who is missing in action. It is easy to lose hope when he delays in showing himself. Philosophers and theologians even have a term for this: *divine hiddenness.*

Though the presence of others might provide some comfort, during this short trek of our wilderness journey, we must go it alone. No one else can share completely the depths of our suffering and our battles with divine hiddenness. That suffering is ours alone. These are our valleys of the shadow of death. These are our Gethsemanes and Golgothas. Eventually, we end up feeling as though we are choking to death on God's silence.

Consequently, we are tempted to believe evil about him. We vacillate between acting the part of the thief who cursed Jesus for not taking him down from the cross, and managing even the weakest prayer of the good thief, Dismas: "Remember me when you come into your kingdom" (Luke 23:42). These are natural vacillations. Anyone who insists it's unnatural to be tempted to curse God amid unspeakable suffering has probably never suffered to this degree. In the wilderness, it is best to steer clear of these well-meaning but harmful people. Jesus too experienced the horror of God turning away from him, the terror of God's silence. And although God hasn't turned away from us, it can feel as though he has.

Though these experiences of God's silence are not our choice, this is one way we participate in Jesus's sufferings and so find solidarity with him. This is one of the ways he finds solidarity with us too. Having hung on the cross alongside Jesus, we will see him in paradise in due time.

If we choose to avail ourselves of the discipline of silence and solitude, of obscurity and stillness, we'll be better fortified for those dry and dreadful silences not of our own choosing.

4

loved into resurrection

When we honestly ask ourselves which persons in our lives mean
the most to us, we often find that it is those who, instead of
giving advice, solutions, or cures, have chosen rather to share
our pain and touch our wounds with a warm and tender hand.

Henri Nouwen

I crawled into the small space at thirteen. It was crevice-like,
there underneath my propped-up mattress. Holed up, wet-faced,
soul quaking, body heaving, I sobbed over and over, "God, hold
me. I wish you were a real person right now so you could hold
me." I suppose being in that tight space was the closest thing to
feeling swaddled like a baby—the closest thing to feeling cradled
in the crook of God's arm.

At thirteen, I stayed in my room for days, steeped in profound loneliness. I needed deep reassurance—a reassurance that
everything was (and would be) okay with my world. What I
desired was shalom. It's a concept I didn't yet have a word for.
I now know that what I wanted was to be tightly embraced and

comforted in God's shalom. The word *shalom* is a deeply textured word that connotes wholeness and well-being—perfection. It's the idea of everything being right with the world, of things being the way they should be. Nicholas Wolterstorff says, "But the peace which is shalom is not merely the absence of hostility, not merely being in right relationship. Shalom at its highest is *enjoyment* in one's relationships."[1] He goes on to emphasize, "A nation may be at peace with all of its neighbors and yet be miserable in poverty. To dwell in shalom is to *enjoy* living before God, to *enjoy* living in one's physical surroundings, to *enjoy* living with one's fellows, to *enjoy* life with oneself."[2]

We all, every one of us, want to be soothed, to be cradled in the arms of God. We want to be shushed like a baby into reassured rest—the kind of rest that comes from believing that all is well with the world and from enjoying our relationships. I can't help but think that's why so many of us, if given the opportunity, readily leap without looking into the first available arms. When push comes to shove, we take whatever shred of shalom we think we can get. In our search for shalom, we settle for all sorts of relationships and circumstances that throw gasoline on the fire of our misery instead of extinguishing it.

No matter how hard my thirteen-year-old self flailed about in search of reassurance, I couldn't find any. So I gave up thrashing about and lay there for a good two hours, curled up in a fetal position. I was waiting for God to come. I believed Jesus would show up because I prayed really hard. I hoped he'd appear to me the way the Virgin Mary had allegedly appeared to others, the way I'd hoped he'd appear while I waited in the field with my brother and sister. However, for all my fervent prayer, God didn't show up, at least not in the way I expected him to.

I really don't remember the particularities of my despair, except that I yearned for a peace that was not present in me or my family. Father Greg Boyle observes, "Part of the spirit dies a little each time it's asked to carry more than its weight in terror, violence, and betrayal."[3] I was collapsing under the weight of despair too heavy for a child to bear.

If I began to feel claustrophobic or needed to escape noisy household upheavals, I'd venture outside in search of an opening under a bush on our property. It was my small space outside where I could invisibly imbibe beauty. I'd hide, undisturbed, for hours. Where I grew up, the northern tip of Appalachia (my years there were interrupted only by a brief stint in Puerto Rico during my fourth-grade year), there was beauty in the silence and solitude of country living. I could absorb beauty uninterrupted. Nothing was ever going on. But the downside was that, at other times, I was terrorized by terrible loneliness, exacerbated by poverty.

Lower Me Down

One of my favorite stories in the Bible is the story of the paralytic and his four friends. We don't know too much about him except that he had four deeply compassionate friends who were determined to place him at the feet of Jesus (Mark 2:2–5). This man could do little for himself. He was completely dependent on others to feed him, clothe him, bathe him, and take him to the bathroom. He depended on others for his livelihood. And not only did his condition make him vulnerable to emotional abuse, but it also made him vulnerable to physical abuse. If some vicious person chose to bully him, to harm him, he was at the mercy of evil. And what kind of mercy is that?

One day, his friends had the idea of taking him to Jesus. And so this man found himself in the center of his friends as they carried him to Jesus, an action that offers a picture of true, intimate community. Because of his friends, this man met the compassion of Jesus. Jesus's words and actions told him he wasn't an interruption but a welcomed guest.

I imagine it must have been impossible for the man to keep his eyes locked on Jesus's eyes as Jesus stooped down and grabbed his limp hand and said, "Son, your sins are forgiven." Jesus's eyes functioned as a mirror reflecting back the state of his soul. Don't we find that we can look at only so much of ourselves at a time? But Jesus's eyes also transmitted the expansive love of God that soon engulfed him.

Gasps of amazement rippled through the crowd. The man felt a quickening and a lightening in his soul. Before he had time to think about what was happening to him, he was up on his feet, leaping and singing and praising God. Jesus had healed him because of his friends and their faith.

There are times in our lives when we're exhausted, lonely, and weary. Life afflicts us. Our faith falters. We are overwhelmed—paralyzed by discouragement and left alone in our own wilderness. We don't have the physical or emotional wherewithal to go to Jesus. During these times, we are the paralytic. We can do little if anything for ourselves. What are we to do then?

We call on trusted others within Christ's community. We humble ourselves by confiding in them. We allow ourselves to be loved. We learn to let God care for us by allowing others to care for us. We learn to receive our daily bread from others. We allow our friends, or other good souls in Christ's body who are desperate for our well-being, to carry us and place us before the feet of Jesus in our time of need (see Heb. 4:16). God even uses unbelievers to administer grace to us. We must let him and not refuse help when it comes.

An Oasis in the Wilderness

Growing up, I didn't have too many people who'd cut holes in roofs for me and lower me down before the feet of Jesus. In the midst of my daily childhood and teenage pain, I questioned why God had allowed me to be born into my family. Although my precious parents loved me and never intentionally hurt me, I bore the brunt of their dysfunction. It's not that I really wanted a different family. It's that I was craving shalom. I wanted well-being and beauty so that my family and I could flourish.

More than a decade passed before I realized God had actually heard the prayers I uttered underneath my bed. The answer lies in the words of Jesus in Mark 10:29–30. In these verses, Jesus promises us, his deeply loved children, a hundredfold increase in family and fields and homes in this age—along with persecution. I recognize that at every stage in my life God has provided Christian mothers and fathers, sisters and brothers, aunts, uncles, and cousins who have opened up their lives and homes to me. These lives and homes are places of refuge and refreshment where I can just be. These are places where love melts away what is not me—the unredeemed me. In these spaces, I burrow and cocoon and ultimately emerge as a new creation. Amid these sacred lives, I can double over in shrieks of laughter and wipe away glee-induced tears. I can also howl and writhe in pain. These are communal spaces where I am most myself.

And when needed, I can camp out in these homes full of love and hospitality, even during holidays. Here people joyfully take care of my family and me. As a lifelong caretaker and lifelong member of the sandwich generation, I am overwhelmed with thanksgiving for these precious souls. All of us long for someone to take care of us. This is especially true when we are doing much of the caretaking. Each one of these family members is a generous wilderness companion who has showered me with the gifts of presence and place. This is what community does.

As I dwell in God's goodness and grace, I am beginning to understand how he so thoughtfully sent others to fill in the gap, others to help my parents raise a healthy, functional daughter, others who are icons of beauty and well-being. For years, I had nowhere to lay my head. I didn't have people to take care of the fragile, young me. Now I do.

Often without knowing it, these friends have served as caretakers of my soul. Jesus has attended to my soul and healed me through them. My caretakers have functioned unknowingly as the healing hands of God. But they have also been cultivating hands. God has used them to cultivate much of whatever goodness there is in me. I owe them my life and wholeness.

Jean Vanier, one of the founders of L'Arche communities, expresses well my own experience of welcome in the beloved community. He writes, "My experience has shown that when we welcome people from this world of anguish, brokenness, and depression, and when they gradually discover that they are wanted and loved as they are and that they have a place, then we witness a real transformation—I would even say 'resurrection.'"[4] How beautiful. In Christ's power and through his presence, we can love others and be loved into resurrection. I have been loved into resurrection.

It is not good that we should be alone. And God doesn't leave us alone in the wilderness for long. Otherwise, we'd be torn to pieces. He makes available good people—individuals or groups of people who are hospitable spirits—with arms open wide, ready to embrace us and welcome us home with a ring and a robe and a party, people reminiscent of the father in the parable of the prodigal son. However, each one of us decides whether we'll graciously receive the gifts of God in the form of the people of God, or whether we'll spurn them. We reject God's grace by turning them away and by failing to reach out to them.

God uses others as a means of grace. Jesus knew this. Even though he traveled in a large caravan, without a doubt, he was closest to the Twelve. And even among the Twelve, he had his inner circle of friends: Peter, James, and John. These three witnessed his glory on the mountaintop transfiguration. And though they failed him by slumber and forsook him by eventually scattering, they were nevertheless present with him on that darkest of wilderness nights, Gethsemane, when his worst imaginable nightmare became the reality of our redemption. In their humanity, they failed him, but Jesus knew they loved him. So he chose to trust them with his life—that is, he confided in them and welcomed them into the most intimate spheres of his existence. The rest who traveled with Jesus in that beautiful caravan also tasted of the community of Jesus. It was a community in which they loved one another in sickness and in health and ministered in his name, even as they differed in their backgrounds, experiences, personalities, and political bents.

Asking for Community and Friendships

My husband, Shawn, and I have moved four times in the fourteen years we've been married. It's not as many times as military families are forced to move, but it's more often than I'd like. Moving involves packing, sorting, calling the utility companies, returning things borrowed, finding new doctors and pediatricians—not to mention the pain of saying good-bye to people I love with my innermost being. The most difficult part of moving has been starting all over in a new church community. Whenever I talk to others, most often college students who are in transition (and to myself) about the moving process, I always say, "The first year is always the most difficult. Don't expect to feel at home in the first year. The second year is better. And the third year, well, that is when you start feeling more at home." Whether one is single or married, if one is not moving to a hometown (and sometimes even if one is) the first year is rather lonely. Moving makes us feel decontextualized.

It's hard to explain ourselves—who we are, where we are from, and what sort of affections we have—to new acquaintances. It is hard to communicate the essence of who we are upon first meeting another. People are seldom ready to receive us in all our glory and our complexity upon first introductions. We are understood and understand others best in context. That is why we slowly, naturally, and with some intention enter into intimate relationships.

One thing to keep in mind when we are searching for a community and our place in it is prayer. In the wilderness, we can't help but pray. But I've learned that it seldom occurs to people to pray for good friendships, the kind of friendship David and Jonathan and Ruth and Naomi experienced. We need to pray for such intimate friendships.

Since high school, I've always prayed for intimate friends. If I meet someone I appreciate and feel that our initial interaction indicates an openness to a friendship, I ask, "Lord, please make a way for me and so-and-so to be friends." I never force a relationship, but if I believe another person is open to a relationship with me and that she has the capacity to receive me for who I am, I do my part in cultivating the relationship.

After enough interaction and prayer for the blossoming of a new friendship, I make my intentions for friendship known. This is how I developed a friendship with one of my best friends in the world, Sue. She and I worked together on staff at a church. Sue is a tall, willowy, brilliant, reserved Dutch woman. She walks upright with an air of dignity. In addition to her brilliance, she is gifted musically. Needless to say, Sue and I are very different. I am a short, not as willowy, not as brilliant, more out there, half Puerto Rican.

Sue was the worship coordinator. She was in charge of putting together the order of service, which included the liturgy, musicians, liturgists, and those who were to deliver the children's sermon for the week. She also wrote many portions of the liturgy. Sue's office was adjacent to mine. One afternoon,

I knocked on her door and plopped down on the hard-backed chair. I asked her how she was doing and expressed my gratitude for her ministry in the church.

After a while, I said, "Do you wanna be friends? Let's be friends! I admire and respect you so much, and I need a good friend." What I didn't know was that Sue was mourning the loss of one of her best friends who had just moved out of state. Sue was grateful I initiated a friendship conversation because she too needed a friend and was very open to cultivating a relationship. Since that time, Sue has walked with me through many a wilderness.

Christ's body is full of beautiful wilderness companions. However, they aren't always aware of our suffering, so sometimes we have to take the first step and flag them down. Pride in the form of embarrassment can lead us to refuse help. Or perhaps fear of being vulnerable (because we've been hurt before) leads us to engage in what we think is self-protection but is really self-destruction. We end up refusing the sources of comfort God has made available through his people and then accuse God of forsaking us in the wilderness. Our stubborn refusals to welcome messengers of grace leave us emaciated and in the clutch of death's grip.

Let's pray for intimate and nontoxic friendships and keep our eyes peeled for how God will answer those prayers. And if we have to, let's take the first step toward cultivating intimate friendship.

Moving toward Christ's Way of Community

Surface relationships are easy to come by. To move beyond brief pleasantries, however, we need to live life together and be vulnerable with those we discern to be trustworthy. In addition to having a ready vulnerability, we must ask God how we might serve our communities. Knowledge of how to best serve those around us comes from spending time together and prayerfully listening to one another. It requires much intentionality.

One of my friends, the director of a city mission, once told me that Christmastime really frustrates her. "Lots of suburban churches call, giving us *their* schedule, telling us they want to minister to those at the mission through a Christmas cantata. I am glad they like to sing, but that's not what we need." She then intimated, "They really do it just to make themselves feel better." Her comments revealed that churches, as well as individuals, might be guilty of engaging in self-serving service. When we really listen to others with the ears of our hearts and even ask them, "How can I serve you?" we will be better able to serve them. We'll escape the trap of doing what *we think is best* for others and instead learn to do what *is actually best*. The two aren't always the same.

Love is not selfish. It is self-giving and life-giving. God forbid that any one of us and any of our churches knowingly engage in selfish relationships in which we get what we want when we want it with no regard for individuals or a community.

Each one of us needs to heed the words of Father Anthony de Mello. He tells us that truly loving another requires awareness. To love we must be aware of people—complete with their flaws, foibles, virtues, vices, and quirks. "It is only inasmuch as you see someone as he or she really is here and now and not as they are in your memory or your desire or your imagination or projection that you can truly love them, otherwise it is not the person that you love, but the idea you have formed of this person."[5]

Brothers and Sisters So Unlike Us

Jesus's disciples were very different from one another. Do we live and love among those who are different from us? We give lip service to the cliché, "There are no cookie-cutter Christians." But I think that if we are to give a nod to honesty, we'd admit that we prefer cookie-cutter Christians. Cookie-cutter friends and believers take the mess out of living (or so we think). We wouldn't say it, but if we examine our words and our actions, we can see that we communicate our preference that others think and act as we do. I like to believe I am not a stick-in-the-mud, that I give others a fair shake. But, like everyone else, I possess prejudices. God is the only one with unprejudiced eyes.

In the United States, our unspoken rules and preferences concerning which political party one must belong to in order to be considered a Christian, let alone a Christian in good standing, surge to the fore during the presidential election cycle. From the mouths of believers I've heard both, "You cannot seriously be a thinking Christian and a Republican," and "I am sorry, but I really have to question your salvation if you're a Democrat."

Our political differences are so polarizing that they can quickly turn friends and family into foes. We cite irreconcilable political differences to excuse our hateful behavior toward brothers and sisters who dare disagree with us. Why is it that every four years we act like rabid animals, growling and baring our teeth, ready to pounce at the least provocation? How is it that Jesus and his motley crew of disciples forged such strong bonds of communion in the tempestuous political climate of the first century?

In the house of the Lord and all throughout his kingdom, there is a weapons ban. Jesus calls us to lay down our arms. Our arms are this world's ways of relating to others—ways in direct opposition to kingdom ways. It's very difficult to disarm because we fear being left vulnerable and defenseless. In our communities, in our homes, online, among friends, in whatever types of relationships we have with others, Jesus calls us to begin the discipline of beating our swords into plowshares. We are called to cease using every piece of scrap metal we can find to fashion swords. Through our Jesus-obedient posture, he wants to eliminate our brothers' and sisters' worry that we'll take up arms against them should they happen to disagree with us. We are to wage peace, not war, by concretely loving as Jesus loves.

Can We Do It?

Even if we've convinced ourselves that the political (or other) bents of our brothers and sisters render them enemy apostates, we cannot opt out of loving them because Jesus tells us to love even our enemies. If we claim to follow Jesus or want to follow Jesus, we have to take enemy-loving seriously.

I know an elderly woman who, on a daily basis, is mistreated and taken advantage of by immature Christians in her workplace. I am humbled by her hard work and by her consistency in turning the other cheek with those who make her life difficult—her coworker enemies. Even though they fail to acknowledge the hundreds of little ways she faithfully and concretely loves them, her love and prayers for them continue unabated. God sees her integrity, hard work, and love, and for that she will be richly rewarded.

Our love too has to be a tangible love, not a theoretical love. Jesus doesn't call us to love theoretically. He calls us to love in word and in deed. Love necessarily involves truth-telling, yes. But love permits 'nary an insult, 'nary a barb. God prohibits us from committing violence against another human being.[6] No violence is permitted in our words. No violence is even permitted in our thoughts.

Psalm 15:2–3 makes it clear. Only one whose "walk is blameless, / who does what is righteous, / who speaks the truth from their heart; / whose tongue utters no slander, / who does no wrong to a neighbor, / and casts no slur on others" can dwell close to the Most High on his high and holy hill. That means that, as followers of Jesus, we must never destroy in thought, word, or deed.

Yet how hard it is to love when others have wounded us! Our wounds do not excuse us from the responsibility of loving others. However, they can teach us how to better love others. This otherworldly love is a gift of God that is cultivated in the wilderness, where our lack of love is exposed and where we learn how to love. But if it's hard for us to concretely love those with whom we get along well, how much more difficult it is to love our enemies. Dietrich Bonhoeffer says, "Human love cannot love an enemy, that is, one who seriously and stubbornly resists it."[7]

Human love cannot love an enemy. But I wonder if it is *really* possible to love our neighbors, including our enemies, as ourselves, with God's help. If the great apostle Paul and Barnabas, the son of encouragement, two heavyweights in the faith, couldn't in love overcome their disagreement over John Mark and so parted ways (Acts 15:36–41), what makes me think that we can achieve relational shalom, a shalom they apparently couldn't achieve?

Their disagreement is quite disturbing to those of us who seek to love as Jesus commands us to love. But what if Luke provides only a still frame in Paul and Barnabas's relationship, only part of the story? What if we could speak to Paul today, and perhaps hear him say, "If I had to do it all over again, I'd do things differently with Barnabas. If only I were the person then that I am now"? We have good reason to believe that he might tell us that their separation was due to his own immaturity—and maybe Barnabas's—even if God did end up using them both after they parted ways. I think he'd tell us that God's way wasn't to part company. If Paul reconsidered his opinion of John Mark and sent for John Mark while he was in jail (2 Tim. 4:11), I have to believe he would've done things differently with Barnabas if he were more mature at the time. Paul was still growing in grace even while he penned the letters to the churches.

The True Measure of Our Christian Maturity

The true measure of our Christian maturity, then, is how well we love those around us—especially those closest to us who are difficult to love.

For five years I lived in an apartment attached to a dorm of 154 women. I was a resident director. Each year I received dozens of bookmarks with students' pictures and specific prayer requests for their missions trips. The number of students who participated in cross-cultural missions trips encouraged me. A majority of the trips were overseas.

At the start of each new school year, I asked during our mandatory dorm meeting, "Who are your closest neighbors?" Immediately, the women called out, "Roommates!" or "Hallmates!" "Correct," I said. "Those are the people Jesus calls you to love." I said that living with students taught me that a person could be going through hell next door, across the hall, or even in the same room without those closest to them knowing it.

I continued the conversation with observations I had made about myself and others. "Most of the time it's a lot easier to love people we have little interaction with, for example, the people we encounter on missions trips." I explained that this is because we don't spend much extended time with them. We don't rub elbows with them nearly enough day in and day out for them to get on our nerves. If they do irritate us or if we irritate them, we can usually manage to be on our best behavior because we know the irritation is temporary. "That isn't the case with roommates or hallmates," I told the students. For any of us to love the way Jesus asks us to love, to lay down our lives for our neighbors, whether friends or foes, we need persistent reliance on the Holy Spirit. We need to throw ourselves on the mercy of God, begging him to help us. We need to seek wise counsel. It is hard to love those closest to us because our constant interaction with them requires us to continually die to ourselves. Constant interaction displays our love deficiencies. Being forced to love requires continual reliance on God because we are naturally selfish and self-centered.

Stability in Community

We cannot love well unless we are continually being transformed into loving human beings. How are we changed into more loving people? Through reliance on the Holy Spirit while observing those who love well, allowing ourselves to be loved well by others, and being open to receiving the love of God. Bernard of Clairvaux notes, "The more surely you know yourself loved, the easier you will find it to love in return."[8]

We cannot love well and be loved ourselves if we are not committed to a community of Christians. Loving and being loved require that we become stable and active members of the local body of Christ. Drawing on the wisdom of Abba Moses, Bradley Nassif advises that we "stay put and be content with our lives. . . . We must not move from place to place or dwell on what we do not have. . . . We are to learn how to deal with ourselves and our environment where we are as we are."[9] We take root in a local community, living and loving there, while also remembering our brothers and sisters all over the earth—doing whatever we can to help them.

It is very important to find a good community. A good community doesn't mean it will be a perfect community. And sometimes God places us in communities we would not have chosen had the choice been ours alone. Initially, none of the life-giving communities I've belonged to met all my expectations (as if these communities existed to serve my preferences). I had to give up some of my expectations in order to accept the work of God in my life and the work God wanted to do in the community, some of it through me.

In the West, we have the ability to choose which church communities we join. Whether that freedom is a blessing or a curse, I am not sure. Once we've found a community that accepts the way God has made us and is within the bounds of orthodoxy, we stay. We grow roots. We take a vow of stability.

Stability becomes a spiritual discipline when the theater seating, contemporary music, and strobe lights get on our nerves. Or when the uncomfortable pews, organ music, and liturgy irritate us. Maybe the messages leave much to be desired or the building blandly frames a Sunday experience devoid of beauty. Nevertheless, we stay, grateful for the many gifts of grace God offers through the community. We don't flit from place to place, rootless, like souls without a home.

I am not advocating that we remain in a toxic or abusive community. That we do not do. In that situation, we do what needs to be done for our health and the health of our loved ones. Employment and other familial circumstances may also remove us from a community. But I worry that too often we let superficial reasons, like laziness and busyness, keep us from living a life of discipleship in our communities. Theologian Dennis Okholm writes, "Stability means being faithful where we are—really paying attention to those with whom we live and to what is happening in our common life."[10]

Changing into a more loving and generous human being is a slower process than we'd prefer. It takes longer than we want it to because our unloving ways are so deeply ingrained. But change in general involves "adopting new narratives, spiritual disciplines, community, and the help of God," says James Bryan

Smith, director of an institute for Christian spiritual formation.[11] These modes of change do not have instantaneous powers of transformation in and of themselves. But together, over time, they transform us.

We might wonder what a transformed, loving person within community looks like. Author and spiritual director Jan Johnson provides a concrete (though not exhaustive) list of loving capacities that will develop in us as we abide in Christ, which as we have noted entails abiding in Christian community. She tells us that abiding in Christ will turn us into people who

- live with joy and gratefulness;
- bless enemies (difficult people);
- don't hold grudges;
- care deeply about others;
- don't run off at the mouth but offer caring words;
- go the extra mile;
- live with purposeful intentionality;
- are humble (let go of pride and do not grab credit or engage in power struggles); and
- never, ever judge (that's God's job) (Matt. 5–7).[12]

Learning to Love Well

We grow the most and learn to love the best when we are around those who are different from us. If our ability to love is never challenged, how will we know if we really and truly love? There's nothing wrong with befriending and hanging out with those who are like us. But if we are to live with joy and gratefulness, not hold grudges, and learn to go the extra mile, we must be open to living among and befriending those in our communities who aren't like us.

We might ask ourselves if we have good friends who are of different races and ethnicities, friends with different political views, friends from different socioeconomic statuses, and friends who are not Christian. If not, why not? We are limiting our experience of the life of God and our resemblance to Jesus if we do not frequently and closely relate with those who differ from us. We need to tear down walls, not erect walls. In our cultivation of friendships, we must be careful not to exclude others. We will not be best friends with everyone, but we must love everyone and discover how to best serve those with whom we have contact. Our relationships aren't for us alone.

The wilderness opens our eyes to the intrinsic value of Christ's body by stripping us of our independence. It shows us how dependent we are on the gifts and graces of God. Most often God infuses these graces into our lives through the lives of other believers. Among others we can better figure out what is good for us. With them we can discern what is necessary for our well-being. We live life together for the good of one another and for the good of all creation. It's together that we live a robust life in the kingdom of God and bring life to others. It's together that we survive in the wilderness.

5

testing and temptation

The last temptation is the greatest treason: to do the right deed for the wrong reason.

T. S. Eliot

What happens when sin spreads through a community? I must admit that I have seen not only Jesus but also the devil standing in the midst of community. I've experienced the downright diabolical within Jesus's family. Serpents will always be hissing about in the garden. As a result, we must watch our steps.

No matter how many times this sabotage of community happens, I am still horrified when it appears that a fellow believer has morphed into one of Satan's agents. Coming face-to-face with evil masquerading as Jesus is the vilest of all evils—a soul-scourging experience.

No wonder some of us never recover. No wonder some of us abandon the faith or cannot bring ourselves to trust the church and its kind. We've seen the devil take a peek out from under his Jesus mask one too many times, and we want nothing to do with him. As Pascal noted, "Men never do evil so completely or cheerfully as when they do it from religious conviction."[1] So we take flight, running for our lives from community lest we be completely devoured. This is a legitimate effort at self-protection.

In Rochester, I coproduced a radio program on a Christian radio station. The general manager once told me that churches were the worst groups of people with whom he did business. Too many didn't pay on time or didn't pay at all. At the time, his words greatly surprised me. I didn't have a clue. Now, I'm no longer surprised. I am greatly troubled but not surprised.

When I was younger, I thought like a child. And for the life of me, I couldn't understand why so many people despised the church; all the church folk I knew were beautiful. But since then, I've been on staff at churches and Christian institutions. I've met the most beautiful people and tasted life, but, unfortunately, sometimes I've been severely tempted to take up permanent residence in disillusionment.

I've grown up since the days I couldn't imagine any wickedness within the church, for I've seen and heard plenty to sober me up. I've seen greed, lust, and vicious power plays cloaked in piety behind the veil of leadership. This reality begs me to shout, "Amen!," to the line from the movie *Hannah and Her Sisters*: "If Jesus came back and saw what was being done in his name, he'd never stop throwing up."[2] To me, it is very ironic that, frequently, unbelievers are more adept at spotting Jesus imposters than we are. Despite mounting evidence of wickedness, sometimes we don't want to believe that our leaders, friends, or even we ourselves could be guilty of wrongdoing. We are blind to our own sin.

Why do some of us casually gloss over odious and harmful behavior—why do we excuse sinful behavior in ourselves or our Christian leaders with the phrase, "We're all sinners saved by grace"? More often than not (sometimes without knowing it) we pick and choose who gets a pass for their sin. We are inconsistent in our judgments and confrontations and with whom we choose to turn a blind eye.

Not long ago, I witnessed serpent-like Christians engaging in a full-scale witch hunt. Their sinister behavior almost destroyed the livelihood and Christian hope of an entire community. One of my friends was falsely accused of not believing something he repeatedly affirmed. Suspicion and rumor swirled around him until he was summarily dismissed from our Christian workplace after the powers that be conducted a sham theological inquisition complete with an already-determined guilty verdict.

Our employer nearly sent his family into financial and emotional ruin because they preferred courting the favor of certain powerful people to doing what's right. They deliberately offered him as a sacrifice to appease these people. Without restraint, they led my friend (their brother in Christ) and his family to the edge of a wilderness cliff. Then with a prayer spoken in perfect "Christianese," feigned tenderheartedness, and a final, "God be with you," these powerful people pushed my friend and his family off the cliff and walked away. The story they told the rest of the community was a fiction, as they insisted that he and his family had chosen to jump off the cliff. In the following months, I watched as this group of leaders acted as though they'd done the work of God. But their actions demoralized the entire community and unleashed a spirit of doubt, fear, and suspicion, as witch hunts are wont to do.

Throughout this experience, I cringed as I saw up close the truth of C. S. Lewis's observation in his *Reflection on the Psalms*:

> "The higher, the more in danger." The "average sensual man" who is sometimes unfaithful to his wife, sometimes tipsy, always a little selfish, now and then (within the law) a trip sharp in his

deals, is certainly, by ordinary standards, a "lower" type than the man whose soul is filled with some great Cause, to which he will subordinate his appetites, his fortune, and even his safety. But it is out of the second man that something really fiendish can be made; an Inquisitor.[3]

In the church, there are so-called believers who will use and abuse us with a smile and a prayer and all sorts of God-talk. Yet, if we listen carefully, we can discern a faint hissing in the background. Granted, such people don't always realize what they're doing, but sometimes they do. Either way, it doesn't eliminate or excuse the harm done. Power-hungry and controlling "Christian" leaders can be among the most cunning of devils—experts at using the Word of God, theology, and people as a means to their own ends. Power can corrupt even the best of us.

How do we know if the Christians we find ourselves among are acting as snakes or as saints? A few questions we might ask are: (1) Does what they say or preach reasonably match up with how they live? Are they one way in the public eye and another way in private? (2) How do they treat those closest to them—their coworkers, assistants, or family members? (3) Do they exclude others? (4) Are they willing to admit they are wrong and say, "I am sorry," or are they mostly about righting the wrongs in others? (5) Are they secretive? (6) Do they have wise counselors around them, people who are willing to do the hard work of keeping them accountable? Some surround themselves with people who are afraid to confront them out of fear of repercussions. (7) Do they seem manipulative and power hungry? These are a few questions we might ask when trying to discern the difference between serpentine and saintly behavior.

No wonder Jesus admonishes us to be as wise as serpents and as gentle as doves! We cannot kick wisdom and discernment to the curb just because we're around church folk. Evil grows exponentially in the darkness of good people's silence. I've known a number of Christians who feared the repercussions of speaking up in such situations. They remained silent or participated in cover-ups only to bitterly regret their inaction.[4]

A Poverty of Love

I found myself battling bitterness after I witnessed this systemic evil against my friend and his family, and others. I was angry and worried about my friend's well-being and the welfare of others within the community. The anger I felt kept me awake throughout the night for months on end. Evagrius Ponticus, one of the church fathers, defines anger as "a boiling and stirring up of wrath against one who has given injury—or is thought to have done so. It constantly irritates the soul and above all at the time of prayer it seizes the mind and flashes the picture of the offensive person before one's eyes."[5] He goes on to explain that "there comes a time when it persists longer, is transformed into indignation, stirs up alarming experiences at night."[6] He describes perfectly my experience with anger.

No one is safe when there's a witch hunt. No one. My suspicions were well-founded; many others soon faced inquisitions and threats to their livelihood. My soul chafed at the fact that particular leaders, who saw themselves as instruments of God, were getting away with such actions because no one was holding them responsible for their terrible treatment of the helpless and defenseless. "It's not fair!" I cried. Again, Lewis aptly describes what I experienced:

> "It is great men, potential saints, not little men, who become those who are readiest to kill for it." For the supernatural, entering a human soul, opens to it new possibilities both of good and evil. From that point the road branches: one way to sanctity,

67

love, humility, the other to spiritual pride, self-righteousness, persecuting zeal. . . . If the Divine call does not make us better, it will make us very much worse. Of all bad men religious bad men are the worst.[7]

Indeed, that's what I observed: the worst kind of bad men *were* religious bad men. Philosopher John Paul Sartre summed it up even more bluntly: "Hell is other people."[8] There's a kernel of truth in what Sartre said. His words lead me to wonder why hell is sometimes other *Christian* people.

Amid my anger and bitter daydreams of revenge, I continued to pray for these adversarial leaders. I was trying with all my might not to label them and dehumanize them. Admittedly, though, I didn't want to pray for them. As far as I was concerned, they didn't deserve my prayers because of the harm they were inflicting on so many. But if I was going to obey Jesus, wounded and angry as I was, I realized I'd better pray for them. Jesus tells us to bless and not curse our enemies. His words sound easy when no one is acting the part of an enemy in our lives. But in the midst of affliction at the hand of an enemy, only God can give us the power to pray on his or her behalf.

I continued to pray for them because I didn't want to become the type of person I loathed: angry, bitter, deceitful, malicious, and calculating. As much as I decried *their* wrongdoing, my internal reactions toward them demonstrated to me that I might very gleefully push them off a wilderness cliff if given the chance. It turns out I too could very well be the worst kind of evil person—a religious bad person. C. S. Lewis cautioned me, "The least indulgence of the passion for revenge is a very deadly sin."[9]

In my prayers for them, God showed me that there's a lot more eye-for-an-eye and tooth-for-a-tooth in me than I cared to admit. I was in danger of the fires of hell. In Matthew 5:22,

Jesus warns us, "Anyone who is angry with his brother or sister will be subject to judgment. Again, anyone who says to a brother or sister, '*Raca*,' is answerable to the court. And anyone who says, 'You fool!' will be in danger of the fire of hell." My soul was in a precarious position. Jesus was describing me. My hard journey from the wilderness of bitterness and anger to the oasis of peace involved not only prayer for my enemies but also pitching my tent within the regions of Psalm 37. Psalm 37:8 says, "Refrain from anger and turn from wrath; / do not fret—it leads only to evil." I had a choice. I could fuel my anger by rehearsing the injustices, or I could actively refrain from anger and choose not to fret. Psalm 37 showed me how very close I was to perpetuating my own version of evil by rehearsing the injustices and daydreaming about vengeance out of my agony over what had been done in God's name to my friends. I too had to beat my sword into a plowshare lest I be tempted to use it. This psalm made it clear that my sinful reactions to injustices could have devastating effects.

If I am honest with myself, I too am capable of get-behind-me-Satan behavior within Christ's community. Indeed, I put obstacles in Jesus's way when I use my own methods to try to attain life. He doesn't endorse my use of godless means to achieve his ends. My disdain, my hateful thoughts in the midst of the conflict in my community showed me this: within me lies the seed of large-scale war. When I dehumanize another in order to create my own boundaries for community, I am capable of atrocities. I am capable of being the oppressor. Every one of us is a Cain with our own Abel.

The more I concentrated on the face of Jesus by immersing myself in Scripture and prayer, natural beauty, and service to others, the more reality crept into perspective. My anger and bitterness slowly, ever so slowly, dissipated. I stopped daydreaming about vengeance. I learned to pray for God to bless the evildoers without gritting my teeth. Mostly, their maltreatment of my friend and others no longer sent me into a tailspin of poisonous being.

Notice I said, "Mostly."

There were days when those leaders stumbled all over themselves in an effort to outdo their previous wickedness. "It's the price we pay for purity," they and their supporters insisted. I wanted to shout, "You're about as pure as white-washed sepulchers!"

They'd been successful in their evil campaign against my friend, which seemed to give them permission to escalate their efforts to target others they perceived as threats to their power. Those days, I'd plunge right back into seething anger and vengeful calculations. It was all I could do to call upon God and others to restrain me from lunging at the evildoers and biting down on them with the hard truth. "Hold me back," I'd tell my husband while in my mind I repeated, in King James English, "Vengeance is mine . . . saith the Lord" (Rom. 12:19 KJV). It became a mantra.

Although this experience severely tempted me to fold up my tent and pitch it outside the Christian community, I remained, while strongly identifying with Flannery O'Connor's words to a friend, "It seems you have to suffer as much *from* the Church as *for* it."[10] I continued to dwell within Psalm 37 and also applied James 5:16—confessing my sins to others so that I might be healed. I confessed to friends local and not so local. I made phone calls and sent Facebook messages—SOS calls to those experienced in saving lives. There was no doubt I was staring down the most sinister kind of evil within a Christian community, and I was in danger of succumbing to it.

Still, I couldn't forget or ignore the goodness, beauty, and love I experienced amid God's people. In some mysterious way, God turned the tables and used this wilderness experience to show me that there was a love drought in my own soul. My conceptions of love were too small. My practice of love was limited. I was love-impoverished.

Throughout the experience, God soaked my soul in grace and began to sow his seeds of expansive love within me. Every now and then, a chance utterance of the Father-forgive-them-for-they-know-not-what-they-do prayer fell from my lips. I never knew that Jesus's prayer would need to become mine too.

It is so natural to love people just like us—people with whom we agree and who bring out the best in us. Even unbelievers do that. But it takes an agonizingly deep work of God in our lives to unnaturally love those who seek to harm us, those who distort life and truth and wreck communities all in the name of Jesus. Even as I write these words, I am aware that God is still doing that agonizingly deep work in me. Forgiveness, healing, and wholeness take time. God often begins this great work of making us more loving in the wilderness—amid difficulty. Until then, we are generally unaware of the work that needs to be done in our hearts.

Testing versus Temptation

After all this, why am I still surprised by the variety of evil that resides within? I suppose it's because at bottom I believe I am a better person than I actually am. It's why I need the wilderness.

In Deuteronomy 8:2, Moses tells the entire Israelite assembly, "Remember how the LORD your God led you all the way in the wilderness these forty years, to humble and test you in order to know what was in your heart, whether or not you would keep his commandments." God leads us through the wilderness to humble and test us, to discover what is in our hearts. Ultimately, he knows what is in our hearts, but he uses our wilderness experiences to bring that which is hidden from us into the light. Even those who are very self-aware cannot begin to know what godlessness has burrowed deep into the furthest recesses of their hearts. God uses difficulty to reveal what is in there and beckons us to cooperate with him by submitting to his grace while he rids us of the evil inside. Within all of us is a treasury of good and evil, says St. Macarius: "The heart itself is but a small vessel, yet dragons are there, and there are also lions; there are poisonous beasts and all the treasures of evil. But there too is God, the angels, the life and the kingdom, the light and the apostles, the heavenly cities and the treasuries of grace—all things are there."[11]

We need to be clear: God does not tempt us (James 1:13–15). God tests us. He tests individuals, and I believe he also tests communities. Given that these are both biblical notions—namely, that God does not tempt us but that he does indeed test us—it seems clear that there is a difference between testing and temptation. It may not be easy, however, to say what that difference is. Perhaps we can say that wilderness testing drives us to God because it forces godless attitudes and bents (sins)—these beasts—out of hiding. Once the godless ways have surfaced and the states of our souls and communities have been unveiled, we can be brought to life through repentance. Testing drives us to repentance. Repentance involves confessing that we have sinned and also detaching from sin and disordered affections. We repent and become intentional in living lives that overcome evil with good (Rom. 12:21).

It is also possible that once the testing of a particular area of our lives or community is over (for the moment), we will emerge rejoicing, giving glory to God with hearts full of thanksgiving because the test has shown that our hearts bear a resemblance to Jesus's heart. We are surprised by grace because we look more like Jesus than we imagined. We are surprised that God is working in our hearts even when we aren't aware of it. But that's what the kingdom of God is like. This growth of grace within us, the kingdom growing within regardless of our awareness, reminds me of the parable of the growing seed. In the parable, a man scatters the seed, and no matter whether he is asleep or awake, the seed sprouts and grows (Mark 4:26–29).

Temptation, in contrast, feeds on our evil desires. The purpose of temptation is not to drive us to repentance. It's to drive us away from God. Temptation is not of God. It has its origin in the pit of hell. Its goal is to lure us to destruction. Satan's purpose in temptation is to undo whatever good is or might be—whatever God-life is within us and within our communities. Temptation preys on our impatience and our hunger for power. John Arnold, Anglican priest, notes, "We are too anxious to be able to wait for fruit and time to ripen, so we take the shortcuts of robbery and violence, even the torture of little children; sin leads to crimes against both nature and our fellow human beings."[12]

The devil would love nothing more than to destroy us in the wilderness and, with our destruction, destroy untold numbers of people and swaths of God's creation. Our destruction is never ours alone. He will do whatever he can to turn us away from knowing God and living out the good and true life of God in this world. He sets up obstacles to the life of faith.

As the father of lies and the lover of discord and death, he seeks dominion over the earth by fathering more children. It's his way of corrupting God's creation mandate to Adam and Eve, the mandate in which God tells them to be fruitful and multiply and subdue the earth (Gen. 1:28). Sin can so corrupt and dehumanize that we sometimes wonder if certain people, like Adolf Hitler or Joseph Stalin, or even some of those we are acquainted with, are the devil incarnate (somehow we exclude ourselves from that consideration).

Our sins are life-sucking, destroyers of life, but they cannot turn us or anyone else into the devil incarnate. However, the devil can have his way with human beings. Picking up on Fyodor Dostoyevsky's wisdom, Arnold astutely and somewhat imaginatively describes how the devil works in the lives of people throughout the world: "He has to content himself, with apparently endless partial and fragmentary incarnations in those of us who with part of, perhaps with most of, but never with all our hearts and minds do evil in the world."[13]

As children who fear our heavenly Father, we want nothing to do with the devil and his destructive schemes. We don't want to sow seeds of destruction in our souls or communities. With destruction, it's as though the sound of maniacal laughter can be heard reverberating throughout the universe. This is the sound of Satan and his demons greedily gorging on souls, as people give fragments of themselves over to evil. It's as if the devil and his demons are becoming bigger and bigger with each life they ravenously gobble down.

Jesus's food and our food is to do the will of the Father. The devilish and demonic food is to steal, kill, and destroy in order to feed upon souls. Thus, temptation is not something for us to dabble in, nothing for us to court. It tries to lure us away from God. Sin, beginning with temptation, has duped and ensnared even the wisest and most holy ones. We need to take it seriously.

Sinful Predispositions

We all fall in various ways, and we all have individual predilections toward certain sins. These are sins that so easily entangle us (Heb. 12:1). I had a student who frequently and freely admitted, "I struggle with pride." I admired her for being forthright about the sin that entangled her. Both of us knew her admission was a step toward healing and wholeness. I think even families and groups, such as church denominations, can tend toward particular sins, sins that so easily entangle its members. In some families, we see habitual greed or pharisaic behaviors. Others are rich in strife and discord. Some have tendencies toward alcoholism and others rampant adultery. It is important to find out, if possible, to which sins we, our families, and our communities are predisposed. In no way do these predilections mean we are doomed or cursed to repeat the sins of our fathers and mothers. However, when we are weak, we might be inclined to fall into sin in these areas. Therefore, it is profitable to have this knowledge so that we might be vigilant and better combat temptation.

It is important to know that in Christ and with the help of our brothers and sisters in the kingdom, we can overcome these sins. God can deliver us from the most complicated and hopeless of entanglements. This might be moment-by-moment and day-by-day overcoming, because some of us have deep addictions, sinful habits we've cultivated over the years. We ask God for the daily and momentary bread, the manna we need to strengthen us to say no to sin and yes to life. And we ask him to deliver us from evil. I pray this often.

Sin or Temptation

Many of us think that merely being tempted is the same as sinning and an indication of the corrupt condition of our souls. This thought has caused many people who are young in the faith, including me, to veer off the road of redemption and head down the road to perdition. But being tempted is not the same as sinning. Jesus himself was tempted in all sorts of ways but was without sin (Heb. 4:15).

Confusing temptation with sin might be a twisting of what Jesus taught in Matthew 5:27–28: "You have heard that it was said, 'You shall not commit adultery.' But I tell you that anyone who looks at a woman lustfully has already committed adultery with her in his heart." There is a difference between the temptation to lust and actually lusting. In this passage, Jesus was talking to crowds who had been trained to pay attention to exterior behavior and purity codes while ignoring the impurity of the interior life. Apparently, some Pharisees thought they were off the hook because they kept the exterior rules. "Not so," Jesus told them and the crowds. The interior life is terribly important. A pure heart will take care of the externals. External rules by themselves, however, cannot make a heart pure. We must allow God to purify us on the inside.

Temptation is not the same as sinning. Giving into temptation is sinning, and that includes sinful thoughts and attitudes. At first, these may remain hidden. But eventually, if we continue feeding them, they will go public. Exterior acts of holiness will not forever hide what is inside. Our sins will seep out. They will find us out. Acting out our sinful imaginations takes things from bad to worse. It compounds sin. It is like throwing gas onto a fire that will destroy whatever and whomever is in its path. That's why right away we need to ask God to help us and purify us—we want to limit the harmful effects sin has on us and on others.

Acknowledging the sin inside us and then doing whatever acts of repentance are necessary will snuff out these sinful flare-ups as they occur. Of course, we can do this only through the strength and power of the Holy Spirit. Acts of repentance include confession to God and others, service, and any other disciplines that will put to death the sin that dwells inside us. When we become aware of sin in ourselves, we must be ruthless. We must do whatever is necessary (and wholesome) to root it out. Vigilance, ruthlessness, and the help of others will save us and others from further destruction.

When It Is Really Bad

When it comes to sin, we know we are in critical condition when we've begun to rationalize it and refuse to admit that what we are entertaining or doing is wrong. "When we want to be something other than the thing God wants us to be," C. S. Lewis tells us, "we must be wanting what, in fact, will not make us happy."[14]

Recently, I've been told of several spouses who are having emotional and physical affairs. All the offending spouses are Christians, and all have children of various ages. One spouse flat out denies wrongdoing. She deems the texting, dinners, and social-media communication an outgrowth of her friendship, though, tellingly, she does whatever she can to hide her communications from her husband. He is aware and has confronted her, but she continues. In another case, a pastor committed adultery with a young woman in his congregation and feels no desire to stay in his marriage. Understandably, the wife is overwrought. What effects will his sin have on their six children?

While these are examples of sexual sins, rationalization of sin runs the gamut. We know Jesus reserved his worst condemnation for sins such as pride and greed and devouring of the poor.

Sometimes love demands that we overlook sins. We don't confront every last thing. What a combative life we'd live if we were constantly confronting. But love also demands that we kindly and patiently tell the truth. We must ever so thoughtfully and lovingly put into practice the principles of confrontation and reconciliation that Jesus taught in Matthew 18. When necessary, and with much counsel from those who have a track record of God-given wisdom, we must practice these principles with the hope of seeing the fruit of repentance in the life of another.

At the same time, we must not resort to pointing out the sins of others while excusing the sins in ourselves. Rationalizing or completely denying the effects of our sins causes untold harm.

We hope, therefore, that others will dare to practice Matthew 18 with us, others who will bravely attempt to snatch us out of the fire by calling us to repentance and reconciliation with God and others. In such circumstances, we pray that humiliation over being found out will not keep us from repentance. We cannot let embarrassment close us off from the life God is offering to us through them. Life is too precious and too short. Neither can we let the thought that we are too far gone, too far down this road to turn around, keep us from God and from others.

Sometimes the full consequences of our sins will unfold. Consequences often involve harm to others and separation from others. It is dreadful to think that we can and do launch others into the wilderness through our careless and sinful behavior. Our sins also harm ourselves. Ours becomes a wilderness of our own making. But God is still here in this most awful of landscapes. He hasn't forsaken us. And he will not forsake us, even if we have forsaken ourselves—even if others forsake us. God is still here, offering us the gift of life. It is up to us to accept that gift of forgiveness and life. If God has forgiven us, we can forgive others and ourselves.

6

careless in the care of God

Jesus promised his disciples three things—that they would be completely fearless, absurdly happy, and in constant trouble.

G. K. Chesterton

I love how Eugene Peterson captures Matthew 6:25–26, 30–33 in *The Message* translation:

> If you decide for God, living a life of God-worship, it follows that you don't fuss about what's on the table at mealtimes or whether the clothes in your closet are in fashion. There is far more to your life than the food you put in your stomach, more to your outer appearance than the clothes you hang on your body. Look at the birds, free and unfettered, not tied down to a job description, careless in the care of God. And you count far more to him than birds. . . .
>
> If God gives such attention to the appearance of wildflowers—most of which are never even seen—don't you think he'll attend to you, take pride in you, do his best for you? What I'm

trying to do here is to get you to relax, to not be so preoccupied with *getting*, so you can respond to God's *giving*. People who don't know God and the way he works fuss over these things, but you know both God and how he works. Steep your life in God-reality, God-initiative, God-provisions. Don't worry about missing out. You'll find all your everyday human concerns will be met.

Not long ago, our friend Dave told us a story about Ben, a South Korean exchange student who arrived in the United States only to find himself living in prison-like conditions. Ben's host parents, professing Christians, decided they'd best serve him by banishing him to a bare mattress in their garage. He slept on the mattress during the brutal Maine winter. He was cold. Mice scuttled about. And his host parents saw fit to charge him a hefty price for his accommodations: $1,500 per month, more than his exchange-student contract stipulated. The extra income he provided for his austere accommodations helped the mother pay for her college courses.

When Ben told his Christian school principal about his living conditions and about the stipulation in his contract that allowed him to transfer to another family, the principal promised to keep an eye out for other families with whom Ben could live. Ben never heard back from the principal even though another family later told him that they'd repeatedly asked the principal about hosting an exchange student. Apparently, the principal and the father in his host family were best buddies. The principal didn't want to ruin their friendship by addressing Ben's situation. So he left Ben to rot in their garage. Fortunately, Ben was able to move in with his girlfriend's family—anything to get away from the bitter cold garage floor and the scurrying mice.

God's provision for us is nothing like the provision of Ben's host family. And God is nothing like that principal. He is not out for himself. He is completely generous and concerned with every aspect of our welfare.

Is This How God Provides?

We are God's beloved children, the apple of his eye. But sometimes we do not feel like beloved children. Especially in the barren lands of wilderness exhaustion, we can feel like abused and neglected children whose father failed to provide or has been deeply hurtful. God appears to us about as generous as Ben's host parents, who banished him to the garage, allowing the icy Maine winter to enter his bones and eat at his soul the way the mice nibbled at his mattress.

Instead of living in abundance, we're living lives of anxiety plagued by scarcity and threats of scarcity. If we are honest, we believe God has screwed us over; he has acted the part of the unjust judge that we have to badger into giving us table scraps meant for the dogs. In such moods, we are prone to believe that the liar, who gorges himself on our souls as he steals, kills, and destroys, takes better care of his children.

In the movie *The Passion of the Christ*, Satan tries to portray himself as a good father. He mocks Jesus by gently holding and stroking a baby while Jesus is beaten to a pulp. He caresses the baby as if to say, "Why don't you compare how your 'loving' father treats you with how I treat my children?" I think the scene accurately captures how Satan mocks us in an effort to get us to disparage God and try our hands at making our own provisions. We are constantly tempted to turn away from God and look elsewhere for our daily bread.

Back when we and others spoke up about our friend's mistreatment amid his employment situation and about other abuses we witnessed and lies we heard in our workplace, we were regarded as infidels instead of Good Samaritans.

It was hard not to feel godforsaken when our dear friend and his family were cruelly mistreated by the Christian institution for which we worked. But it didn't end there. Something similar eventually happened to us because our consciences wouldn't allow us to stand idly by and watch our friend's demise. As Martin Luther King Jr. knew, "Our lives begin to end the day we become silent about things that matter."[1]

Consequently, we were unceremoniously verbally and psychologically beaten up and tossed out. It was a purge by a legalistic faction. Although it was publicly denied, decision makers who spent time behind closed doors privately affirmed the purge.

So, not only did I have to go through the difficult process of learning to love and forgive those who harmed us (and were deluded in their own estimation of grace), but I also had to trust God for financial provision. All of us who suddenly found ourselves on the wrong side of the new leadership's preferences needed God to throw us a rope so we could climb out of this wilderness pit.

God's Way

God is no cosmically cruel tightwad. He's not austere or stingy. He is tender and affectionate with his beloved children. I often think of the most gracious people I know and how God is infinitely more gracious. The best humans in existence provide only a glimpse of how good and beautiful and loving he is. He's more lavish than Mary of Bethany, who spent nearly a year's wages on perfume to anoint Jesus's feet. My pastor, Rod Kennedy, told us that in today's terms, Mary used about $40,000 in perfume. Mary serves as an icon of our Lord, who is always recklessly unrestrained in his love and generosity. Always.

It is we who must learn to receive God's gifts. Only a soul wide awake, a heart tenderized through suffering and sacrifice while in communion with God, learns to receive with gratitude. God desires that we know him as loving and most generous, always providing for his children and for those who do not even acknowledge him. With the same affection expressed toward the older brother in the story of the prodigal, he beckons us, saying, "Everything I have is yours" (Luke 15:31). He enthusiastically provides us with his life and his joy. Father John Jay Hughes writes:

> The deepest source of Jesus's joy . . . was his relationship with his heavenly Father. At every moment of his life, in every circumstance, Jesus knew that he was deeply loved by his Father—that he was, as we might say, the apple of his Father's eye. Every day Jesus realized anew that wherever he might go that day, with whomever he spoke, in whatever situation he might find himself, he remained in his Father's loving embrace.[2]

An anchoring assurance and underlying joy are ours when we know that we remain in our Father's embrace wherever we are, particularly in the wilderness. God does not exclude us from his embrace but invites us into his love. If we reflect on our lives, we'll see that over and over again he has proven that his nature is to love and provide for us.

Jesus offered us his own life that we might live. His offering came at the most exorbitant of personal costs, a cost we will never come close to comprehending. *God so loved the world that he gave.* I sat on the wooden seats in the chapel of the Abbey of the Gethsemani in New Haven, Kentucky. It was three o'clock in the afternoon on Good Friday—the celebration of our Lord's passion. As the monks chanted the passion narrative from the Gospel of John, I was again stunned by God's others-centered posture. When the good thief, known as Dismas throughout church history, choked out his final request, "Remember me," Jesus, himself about to collapse under the physical, emotional, and spiritual torture of his death, offered him what may be the only gift he ever received, one he could never steal: "Today you will be with me in paradise" (Luke 23:42–43).

Hanging there, bloody and bruised while he labored to breathe his last, Jesus also thought of his mother. The thought of her worrying over her own welfare tortured him further. He could not die without reassuring her of his love and provision. He would not die and leave her destitute. Once more he strained to fix his disfigured face downward. He caught his mother's eye. He knew she could hardly bear to look at him. "Woman, here is your son." He shifted his gaze to John. "Here is your mother" (John 19:26–27). He could breathe his last with peace of mind, knowing that his beloved mother would be cared for. Even as he hung dying, Jesus was not self-absorbed. He was careful to provide for others.

Part of the reason that circumstances throw us into a frenzied state is because we simply cannot fathom how God will provide. We feel trapped in misery with no exit. Yet, so much of provision is a matter of seeing. If we could but see.

In this time of stress over the employment situation of many, I did what I always do when I feel like my back is up against a wall: I entered the exodus narrative. There I stood alongside the Israelites, full of fright, as we stared down the Egyptian army. I swallowed hard and turned to see the sea at our backs. We were trapped; our backs were up against a wall. Our Egyptian army was the mob of cruel men (our spiritual brothers) crusading against us and included those applauding the mob's destructive behavior. The mob approached us under the guise of knights in shining armor riding in on white horses to save the institution from infidels. The body of water at our backs was the sea of unemployment and financial uncertainty with which I had become well acquainted as a child. My body grew tense. My heart started pounding as I held my husband's and little girls' hands in a white-knuckle clasp.

In previous situations when I was down and out, when I was tempted to believe that God had left me in a lurch, God had come through by making a path through the sea. Would he do it again? Yes, he would. In my mind's eye, I saw the sea split in two and my family crossing in the grandest of caravans.

We celebrated all along the way. Musicians jubilantly played their tambourines, drums, flutes, and horns. People shouted and sang soulful songs. God had placed new songs in our hearts. We danced a jig as the throng moved forward. My little girls skipped on ahead. We sensed the laughter of the universe and good tidings of great joy for all of us.

Before our deliverance, I had walked around in a haze of depression, unable to see my surroundings clearly. Now, I noticed the cheery faces around me and absorbed the laughter of my children, of the universe, and of God himself. Music was no longer muted or alien background noise. I had come alive. I was again attentive to the beautiful details of life and not just the details of death and misery. Not even the sea had proven to be an obstacle for Yahweh. Once again, he had come through for us.

Still of Little Faith

How easily our memories of God's goodness and faithfulness recede when we encounter new difficulties. It's as if we have a spiritual form of Alzheimer's, that most terrible of diseases. In our fear, we quickly slip into distrust. And yet God tells us over and over again, "Do not fear, for I am with you" (Isa. 41:10).

Back in the Hebrew camp, I can see myself fuming, impatiently pacing back and forth, asking God and anyone within earshot why that damnable cloud by day and fire by night are at a standstill. We escaped Egypt. Now what's the holdup? In my imagination, that billowing cloud and blazing nighttime fire are obstructing our view of the path ahead. Doesn't God realize that?

Because we can't see around these acts of God, we don't know where we are going. If we could just see what lies ahead, we'd calm down. "God, we're getting restless here. God, can't you see we're miserable in this desert? Why are you torturing us like this? At least in Egypt we knew what to expect in our oppression. In Egypt, we had figs, grain, grapes, and pomegranates. Here we have little to eat and no water. Some God you are."

During our employment upheaval, I was unfaithful. I asked God one too many times if he had brought me into this desert to die. In our panic, we're tempted to blaze our own trails through the wilderness. God seems a million miles away from the hell we're going through. If he were near, he'd make himself known, get us out of this mess, and provide right now. Or so we reason. In these difficulties, the Jesus way seems narrow and unyielding. Those who are coming up with their own solutions, the wicked, seem to be prospering. Who or what we turn to in order to alleviate our suffering, apart from God and his church, tells us about our idols. Education, money, power, and illicit relationships are just a few of our go-tos.

For me, the trial is often linked to financial provision. News of a significant and unexpected financial obligation triggers leftover anxiety from my childhood. I feel my already-tight muscles tighten further. Throughout this wilderness experience, I confess to wondering whether more money and more influence would get us out of the mess we were in (through no fault of our own). After all, with money and influence we wouldn't have to depend on others for our livelihood. Of course, that's assuming our livelihoods are wrapped up in income alone.

Still, I reasoned, with the right amount of money and influence, people would defer to me—trip all over themselves to be in my good graces. They'd court me and ask me to join their governing boards, if for no other reason than because I had money. I'd have a say in major decisions, shifting opinions and outcomes to my liking by promising either to give or to withhold my approval and my fortune. I could pull some strings—be a mover and a shaker. I could rule the world, or at least *my* world. If I were rich, with influence and affluence, I wouldn't need God, would I?

But surely that's why Jesus said it is harder for a rich person to enter the kingdom of heaven. The rich are more apt to trust money than God. So maybe I'd trust money and influence if I had them, make them my false gods instead of worshiping the true God. The wisdom of Proverbs 30:8–9 puts these matters in proper perspective: "Give me neither poverty nor riches; / feed me with the food that I need, / or I shall be full, and deny you, / and say, 'Who is the LORD?' / or I shall be poor, and steal, / and profane the name of my God" (NRSV).

Because my husband's program was eventually cut in a roundabout effort to get rid of him and others, we knew he'd have to go back into the philosophy job market. The reality was that there were several hundred well-qualified applicants for each job. One job he applied for had 499 applicants. From a human standpoint, the likelihood that he'd get an academic job teaching philosophy was staggeringly low.

So I made contingency plans for God. One was for Shawn to apply for a PhD program in theology if he didn't land a job. Perhaps he'd have a competitive edge with two doctorates, and he could then apply for both philosophy and theology jobs. He applied to only a handful of programs, top programs that would offer him a substantial stipend. We spent nearly a thousand dollars in the application process.

My contingency plans arise when I begin doubting God's ability to come through, his faithfulness. I start to doubt whether I am really hearing from him. I convince myself that I'm nothing but an impractical and whimsical fool. I reason with myself, reminding myself that history is replete with horror stories of people who thought they heard God and clearly didn't. I certainly don't want to be one of those poor, deluded souls.

And so I talk myself out of childlike belief. I toil and spin and lie wide awake at night and grow weary. I snipe at family members—making them miserable with my misery. I plot my own sophisticated deliverances. I decide to do it my way. But doing it my way ends up making big messes from which I need to be rescued. Why must I complicate the work of God? Didn't he say that he wouldn't give us a stone when we ask for bread?

Looking back, we concluded that applying to theology programs was probably a faithless act. We were looking for alternative routes to what we believed to be the Promised Land of academia. If I had just waited on God instead of trying to devise a type of deliverance of my own, we'd have that extra money. Like Jesus in the wilderness, we were tempted to provide bread for ourselves instead of depending on God and his timing.

Running to God

Amid this darkest of nights, after I tried to forge my own way through the wilderness to provide for myself, my church had a silent retreat at a local Jesuit retreat center. I remember entering the chapel and hunting for a place of solitude that was comfortable and where I could settle down to quiet my diseased soul. I sat behind the solid-wood communion table with my back against it, hidden from the view of those in front of the table. I stared up at the wooden cross. Every now and then I turned my head to catch glimpses of light dancing through the stained-glass windows. Eventually, I settled down and fished around in my book bag to find my journal.

It was December 15, the middle of Advent. I had little energy left for life. That didn't bode well for my two little girls. Six months prior, I had given birth to Valentina, our second daughter. All throughout her little life and Iliana's fifth year, I was in this awful wilderness. Both Shawn and I had to function, though we had little to give to them. The daily onslaught attempted to kidnap whatever vestiges of life remained within us.

Sitting on the floor of the chapel, I thought of Advent and how it's a time of year pregnant with expectation. During Advent, we intentionally remember God's desire to come to us and dwell among us. We are children of "the God who comes," of the God who is always coming, as Catholic contemplative Carlo Carretto so beautifully puts it.[3] During Advent, we purposefully meditate on the good news of great joy, the best news in existence: Emmanuel, God with us. God is for us. God is making his home in me and in you. He has not abandoned us to blind forces of fate. I sat there in the warmth of the simple chapel convinced that God would come. Someway, somehow, at the right time, he would come in the form of comfort and provision.

I turned to my journal. There I recorded the names of families who were in dire need of God's provision of employment, our compadres in the wilderness. I reminded the Lord, as was my habit, that I'd record the date he provided and the means of provision. My journals are my stone pillars of remembrance. My God would come. He would not abandon us to the grave.

God is not conniving. He's not a control freak who turns the screws on us in order to make us do his bidding. He doesn't abuse his children who are at work in the fields of his kingdom. On the contrary, the God of the universe thinks of us while he suffers. He cooks a delicious breakfast over hot coals—feeding us, eating with us, conversing with us, delighting in us. He's eternally gracious in his provision for us.

God's Provision

Once again, God proved he is faithful despite our faithlessness. Shawn was one of 269 applicants for a tenure track teaching position in philosophy. Miraculously, he got the job. God parted the sea, allowing us to escape. It was a grace we didn't deserve. I took out my journal and thumbed back through to December. I crossed out our names and recorded the date.

But what if God hadn't come through the way we had longed for him to come through? It might've meant moving in with my mother-in-law and scraping by with whatever jobs we could find. It might've meant depending on the church and also the food pantry. God meets our daily needs like a mother bird provides for her young. Like baby birds, we are to open our mouths and receive our daily portion. Sometimes God provides through the food pantry and food stamps, through nonprofits and the church, and for that we say, "Thanks be to God."

Still, all of us have prayers that remain unanswered. How do we cope with chronic pain and a dreary forecast for the rest of our lives? Is it possible to live a good life with unanswered prayer looming over us? Would I call for Barabbas if God didn't provide in the way I saw fit? How can we say God provides if he doesn't answer our prayers?

Jesus tells us that it is kingdom-normal, not an unreachable kingdom-ideal, to be careless in the care of God. We can be careless knowing that each day we will receive our daily portion as we pray, "Give us this day our daily bread." We can be careless in his care as we receive our manna moment by moment, depending on the grace of God and the grace of his people and others he chooses to use to provide.

I sometimes wonder why Jesus wasn't a complete wreck every day of his life. Why didn't he slide into despair or lose his mind suffering as he did throughout his life, the ultimate of wildernesses? He was despised, rejected, and misunderstood even though he was the incarnation of the good, the true, and the beautiful—God almighty.

He could be careless in the care of our Father in Gethsemane when he saw the horror before him because he knew the love and affection of our good and faithful Father. He was daily reminded of that reality when he observed the Father providing for the tiny sparrows flitting to and fro, searching for morsels of nourishment. As Jesus knew, if our Father provides for these little birds, he'll certainly provide for us. While he cares deeply for these little ones, we are dearer still.

In the wilderness, we can become convinced that the falsehoods that the demons proclaim are true: "We will surely die," or "Our God is dead, disinterested, or asleep." Consequently, we turn to our own means of acquiring what we need (or what we think we need) because we fear we'll miss out. Meanwhile, God is persistent in whispering, "That's not so. You will live. Trust in me. The just shall live by faith."

Provision may come in the form of being increasingly full of the fruit of the Spirit—"love, joy, peace, patience, kindness, goodness, faithfulness, gentleness, and self-control" (Gal. 5:22–23 NLT)—amid situations that, in any other case, would elicit the opposite. Frederick Buechner writes, "To be at peace is to have peace inside yourself more or less in spite of what is going on outside yourself."[4] We are provided for when God's grace enables us to learn God's way of life. The Jesus way.

Jesus had peace even though he knew he would die. He was full of Spirit-breathed life despite being disliked and misunderstood and rejected. And now he longs to provide his peace and rest for us in the midst of our suffering. Like baby birds, we must open our mouths wide to receive: "Peace I leave with you; my peace I give you. I do not give to you as the world gives. Do not let your hearts be troubled and do not be afraid" (John

14:27). When we are increasingly patient in the midst of trying circumstances and even in the mundane events of every day, we can rejoice with our Father in heaven and all his angels because it is evident he has provided for us.

Provision in the wilderness may look like death. In our dying, we are as a single kernel of wheat, buried in the ground, dying, and producing many more kernels. In a mysterious way, and for reasons known only to him, God uses our mortification—the thousand little and spectacular deaths we die in this life—as a means of provision for others. Our deaths to self are a means of grace for others and vice versa.

We die, laying down our lives, so others may live. We lay down our lives for our friends—and our enemies. At least, that's what we're supposed to do as followers of Jesus. I don't believe we'll ever know the eternal implications of our obedience to God. We'll never exactly comprehend how in our dying he provides for others. But we too are broken bread and poured out wine. A divine mystery.

That doesn't mean we approve of wrong actions or fail to hold people accountable, which "nice" Christians are wont to do. But when we are able to love our brothers and sisters who have cast us into a pit by willing good for them and doing whatever we can to bless them, we can be sure God has provided life in us. All these seemingly little things are evidences of grace. It's just a matter of learning to see them, receive them, and give thanks for them.

God provides for our basic needs. God provides our daily bread, the manna we need each day during this life. But he doesn't provide just our basic needs. God is eminently generous. He gives his gifts at the proper time (Ps. 145:15–16). That's his way. "Every good gift and every perfect gift is from above, coming down from the Father of lights with whom there is no variation or shadow due to change" (James 1:17 ESV).

God is so kind and so gracious that we can't help but repent of our unbelief when we finally see he has been providing for us all along. We are humbled as Peter was when he threw his nets overboard just because Jesus told him to, though he had every reason to believe there would be no fish at that time of day in that place. But his nets were full to overflowing. We should be slow to accuse God of divine madness. If God tells us to cast our nets, then in obedience, we should cast our nets. God's provision may come from the strangest of places and at the strangest of times.

At the same time, we know we are maturing when we become more and more content with God alone. When God is our inheritance, our souls do not "need" anything else. Laura Swan, a Benedictine nun and spiritual director, writes, "Desert spirituality is characterized by the pursuit of abundant simplicity—simplicity grounded in the possession of little and the abundance of God's presence. Yearning for complete union with God, desert ascetics sought to remove all obstacles to . . . this relationship."[5]

Those who spent time in the wilderness grew to understand that detachment from the things that possessed them opened them to be possessed by God and filled with his Spirit. To increasingly want God and his life and then be full of God and his life is provision. That is kingdom wealth.

God Provides Right Where We Are

Some of us are suffering because we've tried to provide for ourselves by blazing our own trails through the wilderness instead of taking God's path. Perhaps he is calling us to surrender something or someone, but we're scared, and so we hold on tightly to whatever is within our reach. And that's what is killing us.

Something happens when we've suffered long enough: suffering is all we learn to expect, and it becomes next to impossible to pry it out of our hands so that we can receive from God. It can malform us so that we live with evil forebodings. For a while during this last wilderness experience, I thought I'd have to fight for crumbs of manna, live a life of sackcloth and ashes. I became skilled at living with scarcity. I started thinking the Promised Land was a dream or a hoax. I had to relearn the process of accepting the hospitality and generosity of God. I often have to relearn.

What propels us through the darkest nights of our souls, nights when we are convinced that God has left us to die without provision, is intentionally recalling his faithfulness. I recite these instances out loud to myself or search for them in my journal. If we can't manage to crack open a Bible or pray or remember God's faithfulness, we must tell others and allow them to jar our memories and testify to God's goodness in the land of the living. It is hard to survive feelings of abandonment and hold out hope for provision when we are alone. Our God will never put us to shame. He will never let us down. He will come through for us.

In the wilderness, we remember that God did not bring us out here in the desert to die. He brought us out to save us, to show us his power, to offer his comfort, and to put to death whatever is in us that is not of him. Then there's resurrection. God in Christ opens up paradise for us and provides us with all sorts of dimensions of life as we seek him. God ever and always has our flourishing in mind. It is we who must learn to receive.

7

waiting around for God

The LORD upholds all who fall
  and lifts up all who are bowed down.
The eyes of all look to you,
  and you give them their food at the proper time.

Psalm 145:14–15

Sometimes we wait on a God we're not sure will ever come for us.

I remember the faraway look on her face as she told the story. It was her high school graduation. She was already supposed to be there, but her dad still wasn't home. They were going to be late. Everyone would turn to see her as she walked down the aisle to her seat. Her classmates would have to shift around awkwardly to let her in. What if she tripped? She fought back tears. He was always showing up late or not at all—full of excuses. Where on earth could he be? She called his office, but the phone just rang off the hook. He had to be on his way. Over and over she ran to the end of the driveway and looked in both directions, hoping to catch a glimpse of his truck.

Finally, she squeezed into the backseat of her grandpa's old Cadillac in between her mom and her sister. She arrived just before they announced the first name. As she had imagined, all eyes were on her as she shuffled to her seat. The announcer waited for her to be seated. She could feel herself turning beet red. She stared down at the floor, careful not to reveal her tear-stained face. It ended up being one of the worst days of her life, one forever etched in her memory. After the ceremony, everyone asked about her dad's whereabouts. All she could stammer was a humiliated, "I don't know."

He never showed.

When he finally strolled in after midnight, he told her mother that he'd been working late and had gotten so busy that he'd forgotten about the graduation. "Why didn't you answer the phone when she called then?" her mother asked. He said she must've called when he was out for dinner (these were the days before cell phones). Not too long after this, she learned the truth. Her father had forgotten but not because he was working. It was because he was sleeping with his young secretary.

As I sat listening, I became her. But instead of looking for my dad, I am a little girl running to the end of the driveway and looking every which way hoping for God to show up. I've discovered that when I am in the wilderness crucible, I am inclined to spiritual panic attacks. I worry that God's gonna be a no-show. I grab hold of anything that will hold me. I fear being swept out of existence. What is wrong with me? I do wonder why this response is so deeply ingrained. There's almost nothing as terrible as this feeling, this sensation of being helpless, panicked, and alone without God and without hope in the world.

Waiting in itself is a wilderness, at least it continues to be for me. It is another way in which my strengths and weaknesses, my insecurities and idolatries are revealed. When I wait, I discover what I truly believe about God. I discover what possesses me and how much of God's life I possess.

There's no doubt that waiting is one of the most difficult disciplines in the Christian life. God desires that we learn to wait well—that we trust him without panicking. Learning how to trust him during our long obedience in the same direction is a discipline we must cultivate.[1] "Trust we put in GOD honours him much, and draws down great graces," Brother Lawrence tells us.[2] Waiting well, a grueling discipline that becomes a grace the more we practice, is not reserved for those aspiring to be in the kingdom-of-God hall of fame. It is something God desires for each one of us. It is a gift of God for the masses.

Andrew Murray is right in saying that waiting on God teaches us unceasing dependence on him.[3] I think that it's during the wait, more than at any other time, that Christ is being formed in us. In a sense, then, waiting is the womb of the kingdom in which we are formed. It is intimately connected with silence and solitude and even with darkness. While we wait, we cannot see ahead. We are not farsighted. Waiting involves using spiritual nearsightedness.

During the wait, new dimensions of the God-life are being formed in us. Most of the time, we aren't even fully aware of what is transpiring. We don't know exactly how we are being formed and shaped. But while we wait and as we learn to pay attention to the details of life right in front of us, we discover that God's grace is "always hidden under the strangest appearances," as the eighteenth-century Jesuit priest, Jean-Pierre de Caussade says.[4] Life all around us is full of nooks and crannies, of delights and wonders—some of which have always been there but we've yet to see. The season of waiting slows us down so that we notice. If we let it, it has the potential to slow us down so that we can be still and know God.

Of course, being in this womb can be terrifying because we cannot anticipate the unknown, and, naturally, we like to know what is going on. It also might be terrifying because we fear that we'll always be waiting—waiting for a relationship to materialize or for the redemptive resolution of a situation. And it is true that throughout our lives we will wait for different things. We will wait for the resurrection of the just, for God to make all things new. God will give us the grace we need to wait for these things. As we turn to him, the pain and angst over the wait will lessen. Our vision and understanding will widen so that anxiety will no longer dominate our world.

In the meantime, whether our wait is relatively short or long, we can trust that we are being purified and that God is increasing our capacity for glory. God uses waiting to enlarge our souls. While we are waiting on God, he is often waiting on us. He is waiting on us to fully surrender ourselves to him. Once we surrender, we can move forward.

In this womb, this wilderness experience, we are being, and also becoming, who we are. My friend Karen Swallow-Prior writes, "For it is in conformity to one's true nature that one is most becoming in both senses of the word: well-fitted and beautiful."[5] The wait is where we become more well-fitted to the person God is making us to be. And the more we are what we were meant to be, the more beautiful we become.

But waiting itself can be inglorious. How do we wait well while confined in the wilderness womb when we feel as if we're quickly unraveling instead of being knit together?

A Hard Wait

My husband, Shawn, answered the phone that night.[6] Turning to me, he said, "Marlena, your brother is on the phone. Something's happened to your dad." I felt a knot in the pit of my stomach as I reached for the receiver.

"Kenny, what's wrong?"

"Dad had an accident. He totaled your car." At my dad's unrelenting insistence, we'd exchanged cars a month earlier so he could get ours repaired for a cheaper price in Pennsylvania. "How is he?" I asked.

"I don't know. We can't find him."

"What do you mean you can't find him?"

"We think he's lost in the woods. Michelle and I have been looking for him since four this afternoon. The police called off the search because it's dark. They think he was drunk and fled the scene. But I'm not sure. He might have hit his head against the steering wheel and just be out of it. I say that because we stopped at an old farmhouse near the accident. The farmer and his wife said my dad knocked at their door and told them he was cold. When they asked if he needed any help, he swore at them and told them he didn't. Then he left. They said he was all cut up and bruised and that he was almost incoherent. Ask the Lord to help us find him."

Kenny told me that he and my sister, Michelle, would continue combing the woods for my dad. After I hung up, I relayed the details to Shawn. Then we begged God to spare my dad's life.

God did spare his life. My siblings never found him. However, he stumbled out of the woods and somehow made it back on his own. But after the accident, my dad began engaging in even more bizarre, erratic, and dangerous behavior. Two weeks after the accident, he quit his job, leaving him and my mom with no health insurance and no income. At that time, my parents were living temporarily with my sister and her family because they'd sold their property and were searching for a new home. But since my dad was behaving so recklessly—drinking and driving, getting into fights at bars, claiming he was a spy, hitting people up for money, and generally acting like a maniac—neighbors, friends, and family members feared for their safety. No one wanted him around. My brother-in-law insisted that my mom and dad leave their home. My parents became homeless.

A reprieve from the nightmare came when my dad was detained by police for a 302—also known as a mental-health arrest. We all breathed a collective sigh of relief. For the moment, we didn't have to worry that he would kill himself or someone else during one of his outbursts. In custody, my dad was diagnosed with bipolar disorder, a diagnosis he refused to accept. Throughout the year following his arrest and diagnosis, my dad bounced back and forth between jail and mental institutions, while my mom bounced among the houses of family members and friends.

I've spent a long time waiting on God to bring order and healing out of chaos, but I haven't always waited well. For two months after the accident, while fervently begging God to heal my dad, I was irritable and neglected my husband and daughter. Meanwhile, I spent hours on the phone with lawyers, judges, social workers, friends, and family members in an effort to help my dad and to find my mom a home.

I finally stopped my fix-it-all frenzy when God lovingly confronted me through my husband. "Marlena," Shawn said, "you have to stop. Stop calling. Stop everything. You've done all you can. You're not doing yourself or us any good. Don't let your dad take our family down too."

It was hard to release my grip and wait on God in the midst of chronic difficulty. But Shawn was right; I was at the end of my rope. The unraveling of my dad's mind threatened to unravel me and my family. How was I supposed to wait on God when things were going from bad to worse? How could I live well while waiting for acutely stressful circumstances to cease? What if they didn't?

When the present is painful, we want to do anything but wait. When my father was in the throes of his unraveling, I wanted to crawl into bed and pull the covers over my head for days on end. There were times when I did launch myself onto my bed just to be still, to weep, or to grasp for a moment of relief. I felt my ability to respond waning.

I couldn't allow myself to surrender to waiting-induced exhaustion, though I desperately wanted to. I wanted to take several mental-health days in a row, as a former supervisee of mine used to call them. I wanted to sleep it away. Or resort to sitting under a bush while hidden from view, as I had done when I was a little girl. But I had to get up for my daughter. Feed her, bathe her, play with her, sing to her, read to her. I had to love my husband. I had to work with students in my student life position. Yet at first, when the situation began, I didn't do any of those things well. I felt paralyzed. Life's undertow nearly swept me under.

That's what can happen when we don't feel as if we have the energy to function, when we're so dragged down by the heavy weight on our backs. If we don't know how to wait well, or we refuse to wait well, we're vulnerable to acedia. The desert mothers and fathers called *acedia* the "noonday demon." At root, acedia is a lack of love for God, ourselves, and others. It can tempt us to check out of life by evading responsibility. It can have a numbing effect on us. As Kathleen Norris observes, it "takes away our ability to feel bad about that. If we can no longer weep, or desire, or feel pain and grief, well, that's all right; we'll settle for that, we'll get by."[7]

Evagrius Ponticus describes acedia well:

The demon of *acedia* . . . is the one that causes the most trouble of all. . . . First of all he makes it seem that the sun barely moves, if at all, and that the day is fifty hours long. Then he constrains the monk to look constantly out the windows, to walk outside the cell, to gaze carefully at the sun to see how far it stands from the ninth hour [3 p.m. the usual dinner hour], to look now this way and now that to see if perhaps [one of the brethren appears from his cell]. Then too he instills in the heart of the monk a hatred for place, a hatred for his very life itself, a hatred for manual labor. He leads him to reflect that charity has departed from among the brethren, that there is no one to give encouragement. Should there be someone at this period who happens to offend him in some way or other, this too the demon uses to contribute further to his hatred.[8]

People in waiting want to do something, anything, to find relief. Prolonged stress and pain can leave us feeling listless and helpless. In such a state, we are vulnerable to acedia. We can come to despise the place we're in, the place of waiting on God for an answer or just waiting for life to happen. Evagrius calls this hatred for place and for life itself. We may cast off self-restraint and seek to fill our emptiness with forms of escape and destruction. And that's when we can get into all sorts of serious trouble.

I think of Abraham and Sarah, who got restless while they waited for God to give them their son. The longer they waited, the more Sarah was tempted to believe that she and Abraham had been delusional in believing that God would provide for them at her age. And even if she and Abraham weren't delusional, maybe they had misunderstood how God meant to provide. Surely he didn't mean for her to become pregnant at her age. That didn't make a lick of sense. What made sense to her and to Abraham (who by no means fussed at Sarah's suggestion) was for him to sleep with Hagar, Sarah's servant. Maybe God was waiting for them to work things out on their own. Of course! That's how he would provide. So Sarah and Abraham, exasperated by the wait, decided to take the situation into their own hands. But we know (and they soon figured out) that impatience with God, disguised as a commonsense approach, proves destructive and sometimes fatal.

We rationalize our impatience. We are creative in coming up with reasons for why we need not wait or why our impatience is justified. We throw fits and justify tantrums. But if waiting functions as the womb of the kingdom, then we must be on our guard when our souls become agitated and we lose our peace. We do not want to become so agitated that we leave the womb before it's time.

The serious situation with my father (and others like it) taught me that I need to learn to thwart destructive forces by functioning well in the wait. I need to learn how to receive shalom in circumstances decidedly hostile to peace. There are those who somehow live in peace as they wait, even when circumstances are at war with them. Jesus was one of them, as was Mother Teresa and Martin Luther King Jr.

The Sacrament of the Present Moment

Instead of slowly slipping out of existence or barely living or living lives marked by sound and fury, those who wait well are alive to the world even when they experience long bouts of inner darkness. We wait well by embracing the present moment, as difficult as that can sometimes be. Jean-Pierre de Caussade calls this discipline the sacrament of the present moment.[9]

Embracing the present moment means being fully present to the now, not letting our minds wander somewhere else or wishing we were somewhere else while performing a task or talking to another person. Embracing the present moment is most difficult for me when I am trying to perform a task. I sometimes catch myself wanting to respond to people online (or actually responding to people online) when I should be listening to or playing with my daughters or when I should be folding and putting away laundry. I still have much to learn and much to practice when it comes to this discipline.

We need to depend on God's grace to help us wait well in the present because, indeed, the present is all we have. Mark Mallett defines the present moment as "the only point where reality exists."[10] It is now that we are to be attentive to God, to existence. Yesterday disappeared like a puff of smoke, and we are not guaranteed another moment. The present, even when we're waiting, is holy unto God. It is where God acts. It's in our wilderness experiences, in the seemingly godforsaken wait, that we must discipline ourselves to remember that God is here. Emmanuel. God with us.

Kathleen Norris writes, "For the early Christian abbas and ammas, both heaven and hell were to be found in present reality. While both were envisioned as an inheritance—one to be hoped for, the other avoided—neither existed apart from every day experience."[11] We must choose which direction we wish to move in the present. Will we inch toward life or toward death?

I remember a time when I was resting in my bed, daydreaming about when God would fulfill a promise he had made to me. For years, I thought about this promise throughout the day, every day. I knew that while I trusted God to bring it about, I had to do my part as I moved toward this calling. The waiting was difficult, and I waited in anticipation of the day when I'd no longer be waiting.

As I lay there pondering the future, the Lord brought this thought to me: "Marlena, your incessant pondering about this is like a student who sits in a classroom itching for class to be over. All she does is glance up at the clock without paying attention to what the professor is saying. Although present in the classroom, she is disengaged and learning nothing, all because her attention is on the clock. She is waiting for class time to wind down because she'd rather be somewhere else."

While my eyes were on the fulfillment of God's promise, they were not on him. I wasn't paying attention to and cherishing the life right in front of me. It was as if everything else in life didn't matter as much as the fulfillment of the promise. My obsessive ruminating, turning the situation over and over in my head, was a way of trying to figure out how God might answer me. I was not waiting well, for I was more obsessed with getting a future gift than with loving the Giver of all things right now. I needed to transfer my desire for control over to God. We must live the blessed life now, not forsake the present in anticipation of a future blessing yet to be revealed.

During his days on earth, if Jesus had behaved as I sometimes do when I wait—full of anxiety and despising the present because it's not the future I dream of—he wouldn't have had a ministry. In the in-between time, when he was waiting for his glory to be revealed, he wouldn't have wanted to be bothered by others. He would've considered those who called upon him a nuisance, an interruption. Maybe he would've fled to the hills to hide in a cave until he turned thirty. But he didn't do that. Instead, he was as fully present as possible to those around him—even while he was waiting to die. Jesus models well what it means to wait.

So while we wait, we do the next thing that lies before us. We do it to the best of our ability. Sure, there'll be some days when we can barely function. We needn't beat ourselves up over it. God remembers that we are but dust, a passing breeze that does not return. He doesn't have unrealistic expectations for us. On those days, the next thing may be to climb out of bed. Get dressed. Make the bed. Go to work. Go to class. Make the kids breakfast. Walk the dog. Mow the grass. Clean up the toys or fold the laundry for the millionth time. Exercise.

It is good to keep up our daily rhythms as long as they are healthy rhythms. They keep us going when the wait is killing us. It is when we abandon our daily rhythms that we become unmoored. Maybe even frazzled.

The Gift of Waiting

On the one hand, waiting is the womb of the kingdom where we can feel petrified because of uncertainty. On the other hand, waiting is a gift of God. Is that possible? I think so. Waiting can teach us to pay attention to the details and intricacies surrounding us—the details of goodness and beauty and the details of suffering. It can teach us to inhabit the present and to pay attention to God and life. In it we see the details of God's handiwork. The world screams his presence in a whisper. Waiting can also teach us to joyfully appreciate what we have instead of despising it because of what we don't have. Ah, waiting! It is the gift that keeps on giving but a gift that not even the best of us welcome, at least not initially.

Waiting becomes a form of fasting from our need to exert control over our circumstances and others. When we experience delayed gratification, we begin to surrender our need for control. However, relinquishing control can bend us out of shape because we don't know how to function otherwise. Attempting to exert tight control over circumstances or others gives us the illusion of power. In some sense, we falsely believe that we can will our desires into reality by exerting control. That notion can drive us to great extremes to ensure that we get our way. We run over people. We manipulate people and circumstances. We scheme and maybe even outright lie to bring about what we believe is the good.

Hopefully, during the wait, we finally begin to realize that people and some circumstances are beyond our control. God uses waiting to destroy our illusions of control and self-sufficiency and to remind us of our utter dependence on him. He also uses waiting to humble us and shape us into people who are poor in spirit. Being poor in spirit is the greatest of gifts. It is a humility that ascribes honor in the kingdom of God, more honor than we receive by manipulating others to pay us some sort of homage. The wait is where we are humbled and where, in due time, God will lift us up.

The Lord says that the poor in spirit are blessed because the kingdom of heaven belongs to them (Matt. 5:3). Psalm 147:6 tells us that the Lord sustains the humble. God wishes to sustain us by giving us more of heaven now. And since the kingdom of heaven is filled with the humble, and since in it, the last are the first, God uses the wait to humble us; that is truly what is good for us and the world. Moreover, the poor in spirit are able to recognize and receive all the riches of God's grace.

Practicing the sacrament of the present moment while we wait on God is also a way of exercising the discipline of detachment. God uses the wait to detach us from loyalties and affinities that we shouldn't have, or that are no longer good for us, or that are no longer needed because we are about to transition into a different phase. In this way, waiting is the Lenten season of the soul. It is a time when we examine our motivations, prepare to receive answers from God, and also prepare to live well in the next phase of our lives. The next phase may be a season full of life, or it may be a difficult period when we eventually leave our mortal bodies. This wait, if it is granted to us, is where we learn to die well and to detach from the things of this world in preparation to receive what is next.

Waiting tempers disordered passions and allows us to deal well with reality. We might come to understand that things aren't as bad as we thought or are far worse than previously imagined; God uses the wait time to develop in us fortitude that keeps us from being destroyed by our circumstances. We realize that we don't need this or that thing or relationship to be whole, whereas before, when we had what we thought we wanted and weren't waiting on anything, we never thought we could live without it. In the wait, we are almost forced to learn the discipline of detachment. In the wait, we are being detached from what weighs us down so that we can "run and not grow weary," so we can "walk and not be faint" (Isa. 40:31). And once we become detached from those things or people or circumstances we thought we couldn't live without, we learn contentment. In our contentment, we are able to reach the point where we can say to God, "Not my will but yours be done," and mean it.

Reflecting on the Long, Difficult Wait

Looking back, I realize God used the waiting period concerning my dad as a form of discipline. He used it to transform me. In the midst of my waiting, I learned again and in a different way that God unmasks our true selves, revealing who we really are. Until Shawn confronted me, I hadn't realized how obsessed I was with trying to get circumstances under my control. I thought that if I could just reason with my dad and find the right resources, I could fix the situation. When things didn't go my way, I worried throughout the day and spent the night lying in bed trying to figure things out. Ultimately, God revealed that my desire for control and my worry demonstrated that I didn't completely trust him. God used the time of waiting as a mirror for my soul, showing me who I really am.

I also learned that if we let him, God uses the waiting times in our lives to reorient us to new ways of being. After I became aware of my desire for control and my lack of trust, I had to repent. For me, that repentance consisted of relinquishing worry and control and reorienting myself to a posture of rest and trust.

God used my circumstances to cultivate patience in me as I waited on him to help my parents. Moreover, the presence and prayers of Christ's body sustained me. I learned that I cannot wait alone; I must wait in community. I learned to allow others to bear my burdens. And although initially I allowed my circumstances to rob me of joy, I learned to look for traces of joy and thank God for every little gift.

Waiting on God is one of the severest disciplines in the Christian life. Yet the discipline of waiting is essential if God is to form us into Christ's image. My dad is doing better, though he is still not the same. My parents now have a roof over their heads and have entered a period of stability. I am profoundly grateful. And while I am uncertain of my dad's future, one thing is certain. If I once again face this type of wait, I will not be in a fix-it-all frenzy. I learned that I cannot fix everything. Only God can.

8

the death of a dream

I shall look at the world through tears. Perhaps I shall see things that dry-eyed I could not see.

Nicholas Wolterstorff

What do we say to good people when their worlds fall apart? What do we tell the man or woman whose spouse has just told them, "I want out of this marriage. I don't love you anymore"? What do we tell the parents of the young children who died in their classrooms from a freak tornado right before school let out? Or the parents whose babies were gunned down by a deranged killer one sunny morning shortly after they arrived at school? Do we have words for the Syrian parents whose four-month-old infant was killed by heartless Syrian soldiers as the family attempted to cross the border and flee the violence in their hometown? What do we say to the parents (and to the other family members) of those who've committed suicide?

I think of Kelly, whose mother lost a long battle against breast cancer around the holidays. She had no time to grieve the loss of her mother because her father was admitted into the hospital shortly after the new year with bacterial pneumonia. He never came out. No one saw it coming. Within three months and with little warning, she lost both parents. She lost her world. At twenty years old and as an only child, she lives in an empty house while trying to finish her college degree.

I think of the fourteen-year-old boy I'll never know but will never forget. My friend Hope met him at a homeless shelter while she was doing an internship. She told me that she sat with him while he sobbed, despairing because he was alive and unwanted. His grandmother had sent him away because "he was eating her out of house and home," and "she didn't want to spend the money to feed him." His parents had already abandoned him. Now the only one he had left in the world, his grandma, didn't want him either. This precious teenager doesn't know me, and I don't even know his name. But I pray to God for him. I beg God for his welfare every time I think of him.

I try to support organizations that will help him and others like him. It is all very little. But it is the best I can do right now. Sometimes I am beside myself because I can't do more. With all my heart, I hope this fourteen-year-old will come to know the love of God in tangible ways and to know that God has not forgotten him.

Helplessly standing by while your life is ripped from your hands is brutal. It's also brutal for bystanders who'd do anything within their means to help if they could. Many of us live with broken hearts because of the suffering we see and experience. The situations I mentioned are what I call living nightmares. In these situations, we had best be quiet and prayerfully present while doing whatever we can, lest our words add insult to injury.

God's Will and His Pruning Shears

While it's true that we may learn from experiencing or witnessing painful situations, I don't believe God allows living nightmares for the express purpose of teaching us or anyone else a lesson. That'd be like saying, "Your child was raped and brutally murdered so that God could teach you to surrender everything to him and to trust him in all circumstances." I suppose someone might counter my claim by saying that God commanded Abraham to sacrifice Isaac for the express purpose of teaching him a lesson about surrender and trust. I don't buy it. It's hard for me to believe that's what was going on or the only thing going on (although in the end, what I believe doesn't change the truth of the matter).

As I was pondering these matters, ever bothered by the problem of evil, I called our dear friend Dave, a philosopher-theologian who has been studying the story of Abraham and Isaac for years. He said, "Whatever was going on with Abraham, it is not generalizable."[1] In fact, he said, in Jewish literature, some believe that "Abraham was testing God."[2] My intent here is not to launch a theological debate or to make it onto someone's heresy list. The problem of evil has been debated for centuries by the greatest minds and souls in Christendom. No one has arrived at a satisfactory answer. And I won't either. I simply posit that I don't believe God allows the horrors of living nightmares *just* to teach us spiritual lessons.

But God does prune those of us who are following Jesus. Jesus says so. Pruning is necessary to keep plants healthy and to keep them from succumbing to diseases. Pruning helps plants grow and gives direction to growth. And pruning helps plants bear more fruit. Likewise, God prunes us to keep us healthy, fruitful, growing, and moving in a certain direction. It's a direction he has in mind. In John 15:1–2, Jesus tells us, "I am the true vine,

113

and my Father is the gardener. He cuts off every branch in me that bears no fruit, while every branch that does bear fruit he prunes so that it will be even more fruitful." The more fruitful we are, the more pruning will occur.

It's hard to think of the wilderness as a pruning experience, but at times it is. Pruning is always painful because it involves loss. It can involve loss of good, luxuriant, and fruitful branches in our lives. When God begins to prune these fruitful branches, we seldom recognize it as pruning. We are aghast that God would mess with something so fruitful, something that brings us joy. His actions hardly ever make sense to us at the time. We may even consider the pruning a punishment or a curse. The pruning experience always reminds me that God's ways are not our ways. I confess that I sometimes wish my ways were his ways. I really do.

When Shawn was offered his first academic position, I was terribly upset. It meant that we'd have to leave our beloved Rochester, New York, and everything for which Rochester stood. That wasn't the answer to prayer I was looking for. For several years prior to the job offer, I was praying that we could stay. It's kind of ironic, really, because originally I didn't want to step foot in Rochester. Before we moved there, when I thought of Rochester, I thought of frigid temperatures, lots of snow, and nothing else.

And anyway, Shawn had a couple of options when it came to pursuing his PhD. Our choices were the University of Rochester, the University of Miami, or the University of Texas in Austin. When I thought of Miami, I thought of returning to my Spanish roots and culture. It is close to Puerto Rico. It is a city of ethnic diversity and close to the ocean I so love. Granted, Miami brought to mind hurricanes and cockroaches and whatever other kind of southern pests might visit our home. Still, the thought of Miami was alluring. Austin was also appealing because, like Miami, it is a city teeming with life, not to mention innovation. In Miami or Austin, we might boil in the sunshine, but we wouldn't freeze through the long cloudy days of the winter as we would in Rochester. Compared to those two cities, Rochester seemed mediocre at best. For me, Rochester was the wrong direction.

But geography wasn't the only factor we had to consider in our decision-making process. Six months before Shawn found out he was accepted into these programs, we received the phone call no one ever wants to receive. In tears, Shawn's mother called to tell us that his dad, Paul, had secondary liver cancer. Apparently, the cancer had originated in his esophagus. The doctors weren't sure how long he had to live.

If we headed to either Texas or Florida, we wouldn't be able to afford to travel back and forth to see his parents. If we moved to Rochester, we could make the drive to his hometown in a little less than eight hours.

After much prayer, we chose Rochester, the last place I wanted to go, because of the uncertainty of Paul's life expectancy. He died two weeks after we moved to Rochester. Losing him shortly after we moved to a new place where we didn't know anyone made the transition into graduate school and a new job even more painful. We had left a wonderful church family in Ohio. In Rochester, no one knew us or knew that we needed comfort. But, eventually, healing and comfort came through the solid relationships we formed at Rochester CRC.

Initially, I didn't want to move to Rochester. And in the end, I didn't want to leave Rochester. In five years, the roots of our lives had dug down deep and intertwined with those of others in our church and community. I had finally found a place in this world. We belonged to a church family where we loved deeply and were deeply loved. We were youth ministers and actively serving both our church and our community through the various networks we had formed. We also had tight bonds with friends and professors at Northeastern Seminary. Moreover, I was creator, writer, and coproducer of a radio program called *Real Radio*, which aired on the city's largest Christian station (at the time). What began as a half-hour program became a three-hour program because of its popularity. The general manager liked our program so much that eventually we no longer had to pay for airtime.

I was doing what I loved on every level: communicating the love and goodness of God—to the kids in our youth group, to the poor in the city, and to the listeners of the radio show. Shawn and I were flourishing. Doors were opening everywhere we turned.

Shawn was even thinking about forsaking academia to be a youth minister. However, after a conversation with wise ones in our church, we realized that wouldn't be a good idea. He had a job offer. Now was the time to take it. The problem was that the job was far away from Rochester. I gave birth to our first daughter, Iliana, only to leave our church family and our seminary friends. I had wanted her to grow up loving and being loved by them.

I couldn't understand why God was uprooting us now. We were flourishing. I was coming into my own. I was doing what I was born to do and had the family I had always longed to have. "God, I have a place," I cried. "Why are you ripping us out of here and transplanting us now?" For a year afterward, I was in a mild depression. Perhaps it was partly postpartum depression. It was hard to tell because so many changes occurred all at once. I missed the radio show. I went from being in the thick of things with lots of meaningful relationships to being alone all day with Iliana while Shawn was at work. We hadn't been in our little town long enough to establish deep friendships. God was certainly pruning me and using the death of my dream of a life in Rochester to do it.

In those days, I lacked the imagination to believe that he could do a new thing in my life and give me a new song in my heart. The days were long. Nothing was happening. I was angry with God—and I told him, all the while knowing I was behaving like Jonah. I had a ruinous attitude. I couldn't understand why God had transplanted me from a place where I could breathe freely and be myself to what I (wrongly) believed to be a completely legalistic environment. I did not want to be where we were. I threw daily temper tantrums. If a ship to Tarshish had been available, I would've hopped on it. But we were landlocked—literally. I wasn't sailing anywhere. All I could do was look back while standing on dry land. And so, not only was I like Jonah, but I was also like Lot's wife. My attitude was hardening me into a pillar of salt. I considered my recent past the golden age. The present I considered the dark ages.

Technicolor Dreams

Like Joseph, I dream dreams. We all have dreams of who we'd like to become or what we'd like to do. Maybe we have dreams for others—our friends and family members. My dream is that my daughters will know Jesus and thus know life. I want them to experience the love of God, flourish within it, and also help others to flourish. I want them to know that our flourishing is intimately connected to the flourishing of others.

And there are other dreams—like seeing in real life those things left only to my imagination. Someday, I'd like to travel to Europe, where I can visit the old towns with their cathedrals and universities. In my imagination, it'd be fun to smoke a pipe with Rowan Williams and other great Christian minds in the United Kingdom while sitting in the same tavern in which C. S. Lewis and other members of the Inklings sat. I want to sit on the patio of a café in Florence, Italy, and see the beautiful artwork I've seen in my humanities textbooks. I'd like to see the Vatican too and talk theology with some of the scholars and clergy I find in Vatican City. I want to see the Switzerland I imagined while reading Johanna Spyri's *Heidi*. Someday, I hope to stare straight up in awe at the California Redwoods. I also want to revisit India, this time with Shawn. I have other dreams, such as teaching at a seminary and starting a retreat center. Most of all, I wish for shalom in the lives of those around me and for shalom throughout the entire world. It's a dream God tells me will come true. And so I actively hope because Jesus tells us to trust that he'll make all things new (Rev. 21:5).

I vividly remember two dreams I had about twenty-five years ago, around the age of ten or eleven. The first one was a dream about my effort to warn people about the Antichrist. In the dream, I ran out of our little green trailer and into the street. A crowd was gathered in the street and gazing into the heavens. (Of course, this would be rather atypical for that rural setting.) Such a crowd would never gather on the street in front of our little trailer unless some ultrafamous person was making an appearance. In the dream, I pointed to the heavens and said, "That's not Jesus. It's not Jesus. Don't let him trick you." But most of the people didn't believe me. I was horrified. To me it was so obvious that it wasn't Jesus. I couldn't believe that even the adults were being deceived.

Maybe the dream was a convolution of all the preaching I'd heard on the Christian radio station. As a child in the late 1980s and early 1990s, I listened to WCTL out of Erie, Pennsylvania, on Sunday afternoons and during weekday evenings in order to soothe my anxiety-ridden heart. I listened to *Unshackled!*, *Night Sounds* with Bill Pearce, *Focus on the Family*, Chuck Swindoll, Chuck Smith, and a show called *A Visit with the Joneses*. Later on I added Tony Evans, Charles Stanley, and

Joyce Meyer to the rotation. They didn't know it, but these preachers and radio hosts were companions in my childhood loneliness and were my mentors. They played a crucial role in my initial understanding of God and of life. I remember listening to a sermon series on the end times by Pastor Chuck Smith Sr. of Calvary Chapel in Costa Mesa, California. He talked about Armageddon and about how the country to the north that would attack Israel was none other than Russia. I wonder if that is still the consensus.

The radio preachers and ministries influenced not only my dreams but also my evangelism. At the age of ten, after I resolved to follow Jesus, I told my brother and sister about him. Kenny was six and Michelle was eight. I couldn't be in heaven alone; I wanted them to be in heaven with me. So one day I sat them down on the washer and dryer and explained the gospel. I was elated that they chose to follow Jesus! Only a few years ago, Kenny reminded me that I did explain the gospel to them, but I explained it while putting the fear of God into them. I guess I was a fire-and-brimstone child evangelist. Kenny recalls me telling them, "And if you follow Jesus, you need to know that the Antichrist is going to cut your head off in the tribulation. That is better than getting the number 666 written on your forehead and going to hell." Today, Kenny and Michelle are followers of Jesus despite my fearmongering. I do marvel at the ways God allows some of us to come to Jesus.

The other dream I had twenty-five years ago was of Jesus and me walking down a grassy path. It was a well-worn trac- tor path in the field adjacent to our green trailer. Somewhere I must've seen the famous picture of Jesus carrying a lamb around his neck, because in my dream, he was doing just that. As I walked with Jesus, I remember desperately wanting Jesus to carry me. I longed for his comfort. Even then, I longed for God to hold me. But for some reason he wouldn't. Jesus was intent on my walking alongside him. He never spoke, but I heard him telling me, "I will always be with you. I will never leave you or forsake you."

These two dreams serve as pillars of remembrance in my life and also as pointers to God's call on my life. Ever since I was a child, I've told all sorts of people about Jesus. Proclaiming the love and goodness of God is my joy. Despite being all twisted up in high school, I wanted others to flourish in God, and I sought their good in God.

My understanding is that God used that dream about the Antichrist to call me to speak the truth even when it is not well received. I am still learning to better speak the truth in love. But when it comes to speaking about God, his Word, and his ways, there's a God-bred fearlessness in me. I am convinced that God has allowed me to remember the dream of him walking with me down the grassy path to remind me that he'll always be with me. And he has been. In these great wildernesses, throughout all the pain, God has been with me. He is with all of us, guiding us with cords of loving-kindness.

God's Strange Ways

Time magazine called Dr. Frank Laubach (1884–1970) "Mr. Literacy."[3] Others deemed him the "apostle to the illiterates."[4] After studying at Princeton and earning his PhD from Columbia University, he headed to Union Theological Seminary. From there, he went to the Philippines as a missionary to teach at Union Theological Seminary of Manila and to plant churches. Eventually, he and another man were selected as the final candidates for president of Union Theological Seminary in Manila. A vote would decide which one of them would be seminary president. Laubach lost the presidency by one vote—his own. When he was casting his ballot, he thought the honorable thing to do was to vote for the other candidate. When Laubach realized what had happened, he was devastated. He berated himself for having an overly sensitive conscience. He could've been president of the seminary. He could've done so much good! He blamed himself for the death of his dream.

In this case, the death of his dream meant literacy for 100 million people.[5] It also meant that he'd write many books about life with God and serve as an adviser to heads of state all over the world.[6] I wonder if he believed his dream had been smashed to pieces. Frank Laubach had no idea how God would use the death of his dream for good. There's no way he could've known.

God pays attention to our dreams. Whether he gives us what we desire or implants the desires we have in our hearts, he wants us to know that he cares deeply about those desires. That includes my desire to go to Europe, my desire for the well-being of my family and others, and my desire for all things to be as they should be in the world.

God also has dreams for us. He dreams of us becoming like Christ and knowing that he is always with us. He wants us to believe that he is in the process of making all things new. He wants us to know that he says, "Yes and amen!" to the deepest desires of our hearts, even when we don't know what those desires are. True, we may not see the fulfillment of all our dreams in this life, but we will see the fulfillment of some—even the ones we've never dared to whisper to another. God will fulfill those desires that are in accord with his kingdom, even if it's in the next life. Of that I am convinced.

Much of our disappointment over unfulfilled dreams is due to our inability to see. We see so little now. We are looking at reality through a peephole. So when I witness the death of my dream, or the dreams of others, and I can't figure out what God is doing, I have to remind myself that I am looking at reality through a peephole. I have to remind myself that God is doing so many things, that he is interweaving the story of our lives into his grand story. It's not just my life and my dream. It's about *our* lives and *our* dreams. *Our* story—the story of the people of God. I am connected to you and you are connected to me in the kingdom life.

In essence, what we really all desire is shalom. We desire for all things to be as they should be and for each of us to find and fulfill the purpose for which we were made. God is pruning us in order to work all things out for our good and for the good of others. This includes the good of creation, for he is redeeming all things.

Living the Dream

It took me more than a year to start seeing some of God's purposes for our move. One was practical: He'd provide me with a full-time job where I could stay home with the girls and help pay down our school loans. Another purpose was for me to use the gifts he had given me to minister to college students and the others I ran into on the college campus where I lived and worked. I made friends—good friends. It was also in that little town, through connections with coworkers, that God opened many doors for the ministry of writing.

That's not to suggest that I didn't suffer while God was fulfilling my dreams and using my gifts. My family and I experienced much suffering and underwent much pruning. I am still waiting to see the results of God's pruning shears.

Years later, I find myself in a situation similar to the one I found myself in after we moved from Rochester. God has transplanted us again. We've just had to move from the little town to a small city. I am decontextualized yet again, but I am not angry. Today I can only speculate about what my life will be like. Who will my new local friends be? What church will we attend? How will God use the gifts he has given me? Where will I fit in in this part of his kingdom? What suffering and what glory will come our way? I do not have the answers to any of these questions.

I don't know why, but in my experience, my way of getting where I believe God has called me to be and my ways of fulfilling what I take to be God-given dreams are not usually God's ways. He prunes branches I don't believe need pruning. He transplants me when I see no reason to be transplanted. I do wonder why we've had to move again. I can only think that God has given us new kingdom assignments. He has work for us to do and people he wants us to meet. New brothers and sisters and others will emerge along the path to journey alongside us. We'll minister together and to one another. This move is meant for our growth and our good.

Recall again the story of Joseph. God gave Joseph dreams. In those dreams, he indicated that Joseph would rule over many, including his brothers. I am not sure how Joseph thought God would fulfill those dreams, but I am certain he never dreamed God would fulfill those dreams in the manner he did. Only years and years later, after much complexity, unjust suffering, and much pruning could Joseph say to his brothers, "You intended to harm me, but God intended it for good to accomplish what is now being done, the saving of many lives" (Gen. 50:20). I dare say he couldn't have said that at the outset of his experience. Do we dare believe that we'll be able to say the same thing someday?

Mourning

If we find ourselves in mourning over the death of our dreams or the death of others' dreams, let us be kind to ourselves. Let us give ourselves and those we encounter permission to weep.

123

Let us mourn together and together ask, "Why, Lord?" We must all be careful to respect the time it takes to grieve the death of our dreams. It takes some longer than others, and perhaps some will never fully recover in this life.

If the death of our dreams has deeply wounded us, we pause to convalesce. We gather our strength. When we are able, we continue together down the road of life. There will be intervals during which we will be able to walk and run without growing weary. When we are able, we speak words of encouragement to one another, words such as, "The LORD God is a sun and shield; / the LORD bestows favor and honor; / no good thing does he withhold / from those whose walk is blameless" (Ps. 84:11), and, "What no eye has seen, what no ear has heard, and what no human mind has conceived—the things God has prepared for those who love him" (1 Cor. 2:9).

It is possible to find satisfaction in God's willingness to put our dreams to death and in his pruning processes. Even if we don't see the tangible results of his gardening in our lives right away, we can learn to trust him. It is possible to encounter God in the space of our dead dreams.

What If All This Is Our Own Fault?

Some of us may feel we've foiled or stymied God's plans for our lives. Maybe we've made all sorts of efforts to avoid God's pruning processes; only now we realize we've made a severe, life-altering mistake. We might believe that it's too late to reverse the consequences of our avoidance of the pruning shears.

Indeed, there are consequences for trying to wiggle our way out of God's hands. Maybe we've grown wild and out of control and less fruitful—harming ourselves and others. However, if we submit ourselves to God and surrender what was lost to God, he'll cut off the deadness from our lives. He will graft in new dreams and grow us in the direction we need to go. We may appear to ourselves and to others as a dead tree or plant that is beyond repair, but our God can do wonders with the shoots of life that remain within us. With the death of dreams come new dreams—even if we had a hand in the death.

9

the God who sees me

She gave this name to the LORD who spoke to her: "You are the
God who sees me," for she said, "I have now seen the One who
sees me."

Genesis 16:13

"I see your suffering. I see it. And none of it is wasted." That's
what God longs for us to know.

At lunchtime, I sat in the university cafeteria alone with my
ten-month-old, Valentina. Her five-year-old sister, Iliana, the
razor-sharp, exuberant, life of the party who walked about the
college campus as if she owned the place (and who many believed would someday be the president of the United States),
was in afternoon kindergarten. At this time, Valentina was the
quieter of the two. She closely studied everything and everyone.
Already she'd been dubbed a philosopher and an artist. I called
her my little contemplative.

On our college campus, our family was a regular cafeteria fixture because my job allowed us to eat there for free. We ate there frequently because we were trying to save grocery money to pay off our undergraduate loans. As we ate, Matthew, also a cafeteria fixture, stopped by after Valentina, all smiles, stared him down. Matthew, a beautiful soul who has some sort of mental disability, worked in the cafeteria throughout the school year. As two of the cafeteria's regular fixtures, we were familiar with each other. I always looked forward to chatting with him as he refilled the napkin dispensers.

On this day, as Matthew stood towering above her high chair, Valentina continued to stare for much longer than usual. Matthew stared back and coochee-coochee-cooed her chin. I don't know why, but for some reason I felt the need to apologize. So I blurted out, "She's a studier. That's what she's doing. She's just studying you." And then Matthew turned to me in his quiet, meek way and said something I'll never forget. "Oh, that's okay. It feels good to be noticed and to have someone pay attention to me. That doesn't happen very often." Caught off guard and not sure how to reply, I mentioned something about how we always appreciate chatting with him. "I enjoy talking to you too," he said.

Dear, dear Matthew—beautiful in God's sight and also in ours—rather unselfconsciously and matter-of-factly disclosed what many of us are loathe to confess: he felt invisible. And for that I consider him brave and an even more beautiful child of God.

Jean Vanier, founder of the L'Arche communities, says, "To love someone is not first of all to do things for them, but to reveal to them their beauty and their value, to say to them through our attitude, 'You are beautiful. You are important. I trust you.'"[1] Through the tender gaze of a child, Matthew felt his value. I hope that our regular lunchtime conversations also in some way communicated to him his beauty and worth.

The Pain of Being Invisible

I have felt invisible. I too have borne the sting of going unnoticed. Unfortunately, being rendered invisible and voiceless is an experience shared by many. I once read that women become invisible by the age of thirty. Supposedly, twenty-one is the ideal age for a woman. At the time I read this, it made me sad to think that I was quickly approaching the age at which I'd disappear—the age when others would look right past me. How depressing. After thirty, the culture would supposedly consider me irrelevant, old and frumpy, good only for carpooling in a minivan, a visual and cultural outcast, a has-been. The article preyed upon my fears.

At the same time, I found it interesting that the same assertion wasn't made about men. At what age do men become invisible, or do they? It's no wonder some women (and now more and more men) go to radical extremes to preserve the youthful beauty they know is fleeting. I cannot imagine carrying the burden of always wondering what others think.

Even though I reject the assertion that being well beyond thirty makes me invisible, there are times when the thought still assails me. It sometimes creeps up, rendering me insecure. I start to feel sorry for myself. All sorts of envy piles up. I start to feel that God loves the young and those in the limelight more than he loves me. As I continue to spiral, I fume about others (whomever the "others" happen to be at the time) being so undeserving of the limelight. I think to myself, "They don't love the Lord as much as I do and haven't been as faithful." I get all boorish with God. Like the older brother in the parable of the prodigal son, I angrily throw my own party—a pity party. I can sometimes be a fine piece of work.

We've been made to believe that having others vie for our time and attention or court our input or sing our praises in a million little ways will make us somebody. And, well, if we don't have those things or the approval of particular persons, we're just nobodies who want to be somebodies. Rejection, whether real or perceived, can make us feel like a nobody. Rejection is brutal. Being ignored or seeing the distance in another's eyes makes us feel hollow inside.

We should ask ourselves if we are ever guilty of rendering another invisible. Are there people we choose not to see? Eventually (sometime after the pity party), it's a question I get around to asking myself. Do we unintentionally and maybe even intentionally reject others? I think of African Americans and other minorities, of immigrants, and also of the Native Americans we've herded onto reservations—people we've historically oppressed and still oppress. I think of the disabled and the mentally ill. What do we fail to notice on our normal treks to and from home? In what ways are we like the priest and the Levite on the road to Jericho who passed by the man beaten and bruised (see Luke 10:25–37)?

I also think of how we hide away trailer parks, sometimes in the most polluted, dangerous, and vulnerable of places. When I make the trip up I-75 to my mother-in-law's house, I always notice one trailer park along the highway. There are no barriers, except for a wire fence (which is really no barrier at all) to protect its inhabitants from a wayward vehicle. A stray car or truck could destroy the trailers and any occupants. Why is the trailer park so close to the road? And why have I heard Christians use the phrases "trailer trash" and "white trash"? Do we invite those who live in trailer parks into our churches and our lives? Yes, we too are guilty of personally and institutionally rendering these and others invisible. Oh, Lord Jesus, have mercy on us!

If we will let it, the wilderness will function as our teacher. One of the many lessons it teaches us is to pay attention—to God and to others. One of the first things love does is pay attention.

Even a loved one who feels ignored and invisible feels unloved. Frederick Buechner writes:

> And when Jesus comes along saying that the greatest command of all is to love God and to love our neighbor, he too is asking us to pay attention. If we are to love God, we must first stop, look, and listen for him in what is happening around us and inside us. If we are to love our neighbors, before doing anything else we must see our neighbors. With our imagination as well as our eyes, that is to say like artists, we must see not just their faces but the life behind and within their faces. Here it is love that is the frame we see them in.[2]

We all, every one of us, want our God-given dignity affirmed by others. We want to receive attention. We want to be valued, appreciated, admired, and sought after. We want to feel cherished and adored—to be "in" with others. We want to know that our lives matter. We want to be loved. That's why some of us so desperately want to be famous. It's why we are overly concerned with our reputations, why we loathe obscurity, and why our confidence hangs on the opinions of others. When it comes right down to it, some of us believe that we matter if and only if hordes of people are fawning over us. But I've noticed that those who aren't obsessed with being noticed are often the healthiest and wisest people among us—and also deeply loved by many.

The Discipline of Secrecy

When I start to question whether anyone takes me seriously or whether my age, gender, or body shape is causing me to fade into the background, when I desire prestige and am tempted to behave in ways that will persuade others to take notice of me, I know I am going to have to take action if I am not going to get messed up. Pursuing fame and prestige will corrupt my soul and in all probability prove elusive. An out-of-control need to be seen is an addiction that will drive us to compromise the Jesus life. In the kingdom of God, being seen and pursuing fame and prestige are not to be our motivations. That's why Jesus told us to seek first the kingdom of God (Matt. 6:33). Perhaps our endeavors will lead to fame, but that's not what we should aim for or why we do what we do.

To combat these temptations, I remind myself over and over again that to be great in the kingdom means that I am to become the servant of all. I remind myself that being great in the kingdom doesn't entail people serving me or vying for my attention. In these moments, not only have I trained myself to ruminate on a kingdom servant's posture, but I have also practiced taking my thoughts captive. I now instinctively call to mind particular Scripture passages in order to overcome evil with good.

Take 1 John 2:15. I recite it in the King James Version because that's how I learned it when I was on a mission trip to India in 1994 with Teen Missions. "Love not the world, neither the things that are in the world. If any man love the world, the love of the Father is not in him." I also choose to remember John 3:30, where John the Baptist says, "He must become greater; I must become less."

Dallas Willard writes, "Jesus . . . , in Matthew 6, alerts us to the two main things that will block or hinder a life constantly interactive with God and healthy growth in the kingdom. These are the approval of others, especially for being devout, and the desire to secure ourselves by means of material wealth."[3] If I am motivated to become visible by flaunting my supposed holiness, by how I dress, or by trying to sound erudite, I know I've veered off the path of life. I am headed toward destruction because these thoughts and behaviors hinder my relationships with God and others. Ultimately, these postures are unloving, for I am not seeking the good of God, others, or even myself.

When my focus is me and my visibility, I become a glutton. Vainglorious. Whether I want to admit it or not, I am inadvertently stealing glory from God. It sounds so distasteful, but some of us in the church are gluttons for glory or can easily become such when we secretly, or not so secretly, make being noticed our aim. Service to God becomes about affirmation, about prestige, or about extending power and control rather than seeking the flourishing of God's kingdom. Some of us will go so far as to use our speech to mow down those more visible. We despise their visibility because it is what we crave yet don't have. Or maybe we mow them down because we don't believe we have enough visibility. In our jealous and envious misery, we want company. All this taints our ministry. In the wilderness, destructive behavior becomes quite tempting when we are vulnerable and so desperately want somebody, anybody, to see us, to notice us and affirm our existence.

In order to break the habit of doing things in order to be noticed, Willard says we should practice the discipline of secrecy. We practice the discipline of secrecy by doing our good deeds in a way so as not to be observed.[4] The desert fathers and mothers often practiced the discipline of fasting. However, in the spirit of hospitality and of not desiring to flaunt their good deeds, they'd break their fasts in order to eat with visitors. A visitor would have no clue that the desert father or mother had been fasting.

Henri Nouwen too picks up on this idea. He writes, "The great Christians throughout history have always been lowly people who sought to be hidden. . . . Whenever you hear about saintly people, you sense a deep longing for that hiddenness, that seclusion."[5] He goes on to say, "We so easily forget it but Paul too withdrew to the wilderness for two years before he started on his preaching mission."[6] Nouwen elaborates further on this idea:

> Many great minds and spirits have lost their creative force through too early or too rapid exposure to the public. We know it; we sense it; but we easily forget it because our world persists in proclaiming the big lie: "Being unknown means being unloved." . . . Now look at Jesus who came to reveal God to us, and you see that popularity in any form is the very thing he avoids. He is constantly pointing out that God reveals himself in secrecy.[7]

I am not to obsess and fuss over whether or not I am noticed. Jesus didn't weary himself in seeking the endorsement or approval of others. He was no acrobat performing in accordance with public opinion or even the opinions of those closest to him. The disapproval or rejection of others did not dictate his behavior; he did not allow their approval or disapproval to manipulate him. He would have rather been rendered invisible and obscure than disobey God. Though tempted to do the spectacular in order to be noticed, he humbled and entrusted himself to our Father, who sees our secret postures, attitudes, and behaviors. He trusted that his good Father would lift him up in due time. And God did.

Moreover, Jesus was careful not to entrust himself to the scrutiny of another human being. This doesn't mean Jesus didn't submit himself to the wisdom of others or that he was a lone ranger. On the contrary, he lived in close community and was vulnerable with those closest to him. He simply didn't let their opinions determine his God-given worth, his opinion of himself, or his actions. Jesus said, "My food . . . is to do the will of him who sent me and to finish his work" (John 4:34).

So too our food, that which nourishes us and makes us whole, is to do God's will. Being noticed is not our food. The approval of others is not our food. God delights when we delight in him, and he sees all the little things we do in secret. He sees when we are not given credit for our efforts and ideas, and he shares the pain we experience when others take the credit for what we've done.

We must choose to do the will of God even if it renders us invisible, even if this happens in the Christian community. I do not in any way wish to minimize the pain of rejection. It can be horrendous. But the pain of rejection is a small price to pay for making God glad and for being whole. Selling out in an effort to gain the approval and attention of others isn't worth it. Whatever reward or ego strokes we receive will be short-lived.

Therefore, when I most crave the notice of others, when I am tempted to clamor for the attention and accolades I believe are due me, I must flee to my cell, to the interior desert, and hide myself in God. I need to practice the discipline of secrecy in service to others. Afterward, I can emerge when my soul is cured or, at the very least, when I am fit to appear in public. I don't want to wreck the church or the world with my sick soul.

Does God See Suffering?

The desire to be noticed and affirmed for who we are is quite natural. What we do with that desire is where it gets tricky. If we sometimes feel invisible when life is running smoothly, how much more do we feel that way amid wilderness sufferings?

Many years ago, when my husband was seven hours away caring for his mother after she had knee-replacement surgery, I headed home to our empty apartment to have a conversation with God. I was really putting God on trial. I was angry and overwhelmed by the problem of evil. I was plagued by doubts over God's goodness, doubts that delight in stopping by to nag me from time to time. I wanted to talk to him about it and felt the freedom to do so. All of us can come to the throne of grace just as we are. Moses, David, and even Jesus were honest before our Father. Questions, doubts, and anger do not threaten God.

On this occasion, it occurred to me that God sees the evil and suffering that occur every moment throughout the earth. He has for all time. Since the beginning, he has been an eyewitness to the horrors that we've unleashed through our disobedience. Those sick and starving, suffering and alone—he sees them. Murder, violence, and bloodshed—he sees it.

This night I was a complete mess over the knowledge that he sees precious innocents, children, being abused without restraint—sexually, physically, and emotionally. I was outraged because he wasn't intervening when he could. Why didn't he stop sickness, death, and destruction? How could he allow those who proclaim his name to be guilty of genocide or doing nothing about it (including Christians in Nazi Germany and Rwanda)? I lamented the cover-up and abuse that happens in the church. And I wondered why I had the good fortune of being born in America and thus wealthier than most in the world. "It seems all so scandalous, God," I said. "You scandalize me. This knowledge is too much for me. I can't bear it."

"And what about those innocent, suffering children who've never heard the gospel?" I asked. "They've lived in hell on earth, and when they die, they're going straight to hell?" I didn't physically shake my fists, but that's what I was doing to God. "And what about the severely mentally disabled, God, those who can't understand and assent to the gospel?" The night started out with anguish over God seeing abuse and seemingly doing nothing about it. It blew up into anger and despair over the problem of evil.

I sat stewing for a long time. And all I heard was silence.

Eventually, thoughts about God's suffering began to trickle into my understanding. I thought about how Jesus endured unimaginable suffering on earth and how God still suffers by what he sees. I couldn't accuse him of not empathizing with my suffering or the suffering of others. The more I thought about it, the more I realized that I'll never comprehend his suffering. God suffers. Our God suffers. He suffers with you and me and the millions we don't see.

As I sat for what seemed like forty days and forty nights, I sensed God speaking to me, not audibly but speaking to me nonetheless. "Marlena, tell me, how do you know what I am doing throughout the earth? You see death, destruction, violence, illness, and perversion on the news. But the good doesn't get reported. All throughout the earth, in every corner of the globe, my people are overcoming evil with good. I send my people, and even those who do not believe in me, as instruments of grace."

"What about those who've never heard the gospel? What about them?" I asked. "What chance do they have, Lord?"

"Haven't you heard about Muslims in closed countries having dreams and visions of me and then following me? I care more about my children than you can imagine, Marlena."

God's answers to me were like lullabies. He soothed my overwrought, hurting soul with the knowledge that he does indeed see. He sees much more than I will ever see. His loving-kindness toward all he has made, especially the bruised reeds in the world, is deeper than I can fathom. I, however, have limited loving-kindness and limited understanding. I am limited in vision. That night God didn't answer all my questions about the problem of evil. I still struggle with doubts. But that night I was thoroughly convinced of the inexplicable love and goodness of God. I was convinced that he sees and he acts on our behalf in the midst of evil and suffering. I was also convinced that he will judge rightly and fairly. I've remained convinced of that to this day.

Our theologies don't have all the answers. Mysteries remain— especially when it comes to the problem of evil. But this too is a mystery: God is full of creative goodness, compassion, and love. He wants to use *us* to overcome evil with good. That's what Dallas Willard calls the "divine conspiracy"—us, with God and through God, overcoming evil with good wherever we are. In *The Lord of the Rings*, Gandalf says, "It is not our part to master all the tides of the world, but to do what is in us for the succour of those years wherein we are set, uprooting the evil in the fields that we know, so that those who live after us may have clean earth to till. What weather they shall have is not ours to rule."[8]

We can become a part of overcoming evil with good in our own spheres and by lending whatever kind of a hand we can to those in other spheres. Indeed, one way we know that God sees us is through others. And one way others know that God sees them is through us. We become part of God's seeing, God's eyes. And we impart a God's-eye view to the world.

The God Who Sees Me

I am struck by how Jesus inhabited the presence of others. He noticed them. No one got past him. His visual acuity and attentiveness to those who crossed his path were unmatched. Jesus never had an "I can't be bothered with you" attitude. As he walked through Jericho, he happened upon Zacchaeus up in the sycamore tree. Jesus looked up at Zacchaeus looking down at him. Jesus not only noticed Zacchaeus but also saw Zacchaeus for who he was—a deeply loved, lost (and now found) son of Abraham (Luke 19:2–10). Jesus revealed to Zacchaeus his beauty and his worth.

Jesus noticed not only Zacchaeus but many others as well. He stopped his journey to heal Jairus's daughter after a hemorrhaging woman, whose physical malady rendered her invisible and untouchable, touched his robe. Among the people Jesus saw were women, lepers, blind men, the demon possessed, and prostitutes. Back then, Jesus—God incarnate—scandalized the crowds, especially the self-righteous, by seeing those that others failed to see or chose not to see. Today, he'd scandalize us too. Thankfully, he doesn't consult us about when and where and upon whom to shower his grace.

We should never put too much distance between ourselves and the religious people of Jesus's day. We too, if we are honest, believe some people are undeserving of God's rapt attention— those we believe are "less than." Frankly, there are people to whom we wish God would not give his attention at all. We are envious of his generous attention (Matt. 20:15). We need to realize that there will always be people God sees and chooses to see whom we refuse to see. Even the best of us deceive ourselves if we believe our eyesight is without prejudice. Only God has purely unprejudiced eyes.

While on earth, Jesus cultivated his eyesight, his capacity for paying attention. He learned from the best. Our heavenly Father taught him how to see. In John 5:19, Jesus tells us, "Very truly I tell you, the Son can do nothing by himself; he can do only what *he sees his Father doing*, because whatever the Father does the Son also does" (emphasis mine). Jesus paid attention to our Father's way—our Father's way of being and doing. Consequently, he absorbed those ways into himself. Jesus is the God who sees.

The God Who Sees Me was the name given to God in the ancient times by Hagar, Abraham and Sarah's slave (see Gen. 16). After Hagar became pregnant with Abraham's child (after having slept with Abraham at Sarah's urging), she began to despise Sarah, Abraham's wife. Sarah in turn began to mistreat Hagar. When Hagar could bear it no longer, she fled to the desert and sat by a well. But God fled to the desert after her. The angel of the Lord saw Hagar in her distress and tenderly inquired after her and her welfare.

There in the desert Hagar became aware that God wasn't blind to her suffering even though she was a woman and a slave—mere property. In the unforgiving desert, God blessed Hagar. He told her, "I will increase your descendants so much that they will be too numerous to count" (Gen. 16:10). No, she wouldn't die in the desert. This wasn't her bitter end. Life would teem forth from her, a mistreated slave. She would be the mother of nations. In this desert, Hagar saw God seeing her.

Do we see God seeing us in our deserts?

Hagar, overwhelmed by the goodness and kindness of God, uttered these words in astonished gratitude: "You are the God who sees me. . . . I have now seen the One who sees me" (Gen. 16:13). Thus, she named him the God Who Sees Me.

God always shows up in the desert. He sees all things, including the things I don't want to see about myself or others. He is the God who sees pain, every form of hideous suffering, and evil. He sees our suffering and comes to us. He pays attention. We, however, are not always aware of his presence or his keen eyesight. At times, circumstances or our own internal states cloud our view.

A few years ago, we were staying with friends in Rochester, New York, for Shawn's graduation from his doctoral studies program. Before we departed, Shawn and I decided to head east along Lake Ontario to one of our favorite places: Bob Foreman Park in the tiny town of Pultneyville, New York. It's a beautiful public park where one can enjoy Lake Ontario up close. I used to fall asleep under a tree as I listened to the water lapping the shore after I had put down whatever book I was reading at the time. Shawn did too. We especially wanted my mother-in-law and our then three-year-old daughter, Iliana, who were with us, to see our sacred space.

It was a balmy sixty degrees in mid-May and the sunniest of days. As we left the city to drive onto the Seaway Trail, we noticed something peculiar. Even though it was one o'clock in the afternoon, it was foggy. We couldn't see the lake to our left. In fact, we couldn't see anything. We could barely see the road right in front of us. We were sorely disappointed. However, we kept driving because we thought the fog surely would lift by the time we arrived at the park. Moreover, the knowledge that we wouldn't be traveling this way again soon strengthened our resolve to keep going.

After some tense navigation, we arrived. From the parking lot, we always had a spectacular view of the blue expanse. Not this day. Our visibility was about two feet. We couldn't see more than three feet from the water's edge, though we could hear the lake. Shawn, Iliana, and Grandma continued down to the nearly invisible shore to skip rocks in the fog. I decided to sit down on a bench and contemplate the water I couldn't see.

I was troubled by the thought that I couldn't see beautiful Lake Ontario even though it was right in front of me. Similarly, sometimes we cannot see God even though he is right in front of us. We may have to wait for the spiritual fog to burn off, the fog of confusion or disillusionment. Then we'll be able to see.

One day we'll see God and reality much more clearly, even if it's from the vantage point of the other side of eternal life. Until then, as the knowledge that we are deeply beloved children of God makes its home deep within us, it will still the insecurities that drive us to be noticed in illegitimate ways. Even in the wilderness, our confidence in God's character will solidify the more we come to know him. And even though we will probably never have a satisfactory answer to the problem of evil, we can be comforted and confident in the knowledge that there is no darkness in God—only light and life and goodness. God is the God who sees and cares and who will make all things right. In the meantime, he desires to use us to overcome the evil we see with good.

wilderness

gifts

$\downarrow$

10

weak and wise athletes of God

Humility is throwing oneself away in complete concentration on something or someone else.

Madeleine L'Engle

Sometimes I banter with God. Every now and then, I'll tease him, telling him that since he disciplines the children he loves (Heb. 12:6), he must *really* love me because he often disciplines me by driving me into the desert and allowing me to spend long periods of time there. Other times, I wonder aloud to him about whether I am as stubborn and as stiff-necked as the Israelites. I'd like to think I am not, but then I'd be kidding myself. Maybe he's trying to break me of my stubbornness *and* (as he did with Moses) trying to form me into one of the most humble people on earth by making me at home in the desert. I can't get away with anything, not a single thing. The Lord won't let me get away with a single un-Christlike disposition, behavior, or thought—not for long anyway.

The Holy Spirit is intent on immediately convicting me and calling me to repentance. Of course, that's not unique to me. All of us are called to repent immediately and make things right, even if it's uncomfortable. All of us become more sensitive to the Holy Spirit the longer we walk with God. Can't God just cut us some slack when it comes to immediate conviction of wrongdoing and repentance in the little things? That's a thought I have when I'm in a foul mood and don't feel like repenting and reconciling right away, even though I know I have to if I am to keep destruction in myself and in the world at bay. As I tell our little girls, "We must obey right away."

God is continually calling me (and every one of us) to take up the cross of obedience. In God's hands, crosses that are considered instruments of death become instruments of life-giving grace and conduits of shalom. Of course, few of us look forward to taking up our crosses daily and dying a thousand deaths to self in the span of a lifetime. Need we be reminded again that such dying *is* the Jesus way? In *The Cost of Discipleship*, Dietrich Bonhoeffer said that the call to discipleship is the call to die.[1] The wisdom of God teaches us that we must die these deaths so that we might live.

Every time we refuse to die to the godless self, the life of God in us weakens. The process of dying to ourselves takes a lot out of us. We vacillate between putting to death the deeds of the flesh (in obedience to God) and hanging on to familiar death. We panic, and then we rationalize our decisions to cling to the unredeemed parts of ourselves. Sometimes we hesitate and decide we want to keep the godless parts of us alive after all. We don't like to die even when it's good for us.

We cling to the unredeemed parts of ourselves out of fear and because doing so is what we know. We don't have enough of a God-bathed imagination to imagine anything else. We are scared of the uncertainty involved in surrendering to God. But as we learn to become completely dependent on God, who has always shown himself to be trustworthy, we learn to stop fighting the demise of godlessness in us, like a restless child who finally stops fighting sleep. As we confess our sins and waywardness and put to death the deeds of the flesh, trusted others function as pallbearers at our "death of self" funeral. Together with us, our friendly pallbearers bid adieu to the old, rebellious us. With us, they bid good riddance to what unleashes destruction in the world. We don't shed any tears.

Because we are at our weakest in the desert, the desert experience almost forces us to practice becoming utterly dependent on God, as we should always be. When we are submissive to him in our dying to self, we can be submissive to him in the ways and means of resurrection life. Yet we must keep in mind that each death and resurrection is unique. Just when we think we've got dying to self down pat, we must relearn mortification. Dying is never easy. Still, after much practice, dying to self becomes easier. Maybe it's because we finally come to terms with the reality that we have to die in order to live. There's no way around it. John Chryssavgis writes, "The more involved our exposure to the way of the cross, the more intense our experience of the light of resurrection."[2]

Although it is quite bewildering and counterintuitive, as we are submissive to God and his ways amid our weaknesses (including our death to self), we are growing spiritual muscles and becoming strong. We are becoming whole. This truth of God—that at our weakest points we are strongest—can seem like such foolishness to us. Nevertheless, it is in this weakened state of death and dying that we are most powerful. It's in our weaknesses that God's strength is revealed. That is why the apostle Paul could say:

> But he said to me, "My grace is sufficient for you, for my power
> is made perfect in weakness." Therefore I will boast all the more

gladly about my weaknesses, so that Christ's power may rest on me. That is why, for Christ's sake, I delight in weaknesses, in insults, in hardships, in persecutions, in difficulties. For when I am weak, then I am strong. (2 Cor. 12:9–11)

Like the desert fathers and mothers, we become athletes of God as we throw ourselves upon the grace and mercy of our loving God and submissively obey him in our weakest moments. The wisdom of the desert, the wisdom of God, teaches us that those skilled in dying to themselves are athletes of God and the most powerful souls in existence.

Dying Yet Again

After one of the most harrowing wildernesses of my life, one I had almost started to believe would be a never-ending wilderness, I told my small group that one of the benefits of my experience was that I had become skilled in maneuvering my shield of faith. I had learned how to protect myself against the enemy's fiery darts, those incessant missiles that streamed in from all sides. I had also learned how to draw the sword of the Spirit (God's Word). I had announced "*en garde*" to the enemy so many times and had sent up so many prayers for myself and others that I'd had my fill of spiritual sword fighting.

I concluded that I had performed my share of the athletic and militaristic feats necessary to protect myself and others from the enemy's onslaught. I felt like a spiritual athlete, like one of David's mighty men of old, except I was a woman. The entire year during our workplace upheaval, I had used and developed spiritual muscles I didn't know existed. Maybe that's how the church fathers and mothers in the desert, the quintessential spiritual athletes, felt in their battles against the demons that attacked them.

While demons certainly do not lurk around every corner, and we cannot blame them for all our woes, many of us forget that we do not battle against flesh and blood alone. Every so often, I have to remind myself of that reality. The universe is full of all sorts of good and bad sentient beings—not just human beings. On the one hand, the evil beings are bent on working woe, on stealing, killing, and destroying the earth and everything in it. On the other hand, God's angels, the messengers of salvation, do our Father's bidding and toil on our behalf. As we lean on God and his messengers of grace during our desert experiences, we develop the power and endurance to withstand the enemy. Our experiences become a form of spiritual weight lifting.

Just when I thought my recent deployment to the desert and muscle-building exercises were over, the doctor found nodules on my thyroid during a checkup. I would need a biopsy to determine whether I had thyroid cancer. The mind races when one hears the word *cancer*. Immediately, I wondered whether this would be my end—my last great wilderness. "What if I have only six months to live?" I wondered. "Who will take care of my little girls? How will Shawn manage?" I mourned what could be my end. "There's so much I still want to do. I want to see my little girls grow up. I want to be with them and with Shawn."

Dying from cancer now—after a year that required me to tap into what felt like every ounce of the grace God had available for me—was not what I needed. It's not what anyone needs. But then again, death is seldom welcome or convenient. It always seems unnatural. But, of course, I am not immune to it, nor do I think I get to escape it. Plenty of people, including children, die before we believe it's their time. Some never even get a chance to live at all—all because the world isn't the way it should be.

After I was told I'd need a biopsy, I went home. The rest of the day was a blur. Shawn was away at a conference. I didn't want to tell him about my ordeal, because I didn't want to send him into a downward spiral of worry while he was out of town. No, I'd wait a few days until he got home, where we could fight worry together. After I put the girls to bed, I was alone for the night. Finally, I had some time to myself to think about the news I had received earlier that day.

I felt like Job.

Yes, there are millions who've suffered worse than I have, but in my own way I've become familiar with suffering and difficult circumstances. Until this point, my body had remained unscathed. The thought that my body could turn against me left me feeling profoundly helpless and vulnerable. If my body betrayed me, there was little I could do about it. If I had cancer, I had cancer. I couldn't wish it away, and I had no guarantee that things would turn out well for me. That night, I entered Gethsemane. Although I didn't sweat drops of blood as Jesus did, my soul did sweat bullets. I looked up "thyroid cancer" on the internet. Perhaps equipping myself with information would give me a measure of control. I found out that for the most part thyroid cancer is slow growing and treatable—that is, unless I had anaplastic thyroid cancer. In that case, it'd most likely prove fatal. Barring a miracle, I'd be a goner.

That night I battled to believe everything I confessed to believe about God and life in the kingdom. Shortly after midnight I conceded I was still safe in the kingdom of God because it is the safest place to be (as I once heard Dallas Willard say). If I had cancer, even the worst form of thyroid cancer, and would soon be no more on this side of eternal life, my family would still remain in God's good hands. I had come to the point where I could murmur, "Your will be done," and release the outcome to God.

Every day thereafter, there was not a single ounce of worry manifest in my body. My muscles didn't tighten, nor did I lose sleep over the possibility of having cancer. Standing back and considering my response, I was amazed at my tranquility. Shawn was amazed at my tranquility. I would have to wait several months for the biopsy because an ultrasound had revealed that the nodules were too tiny for the doctors to obtain an accurate specimen. I'd have to wait for the nodules to grow. A large enough specimen would allow the doctors to accurately determine whether the nodules were malignant.

Even so, God's peace that passes understanding had descended upon me like the Holy Spirit dove descended upon Jesus when he was baptized. This is a supernatural peace in the midst of the most grievous circumstances. And it's available to all of us, not just to me. God is generous with his gifts. Our ability to endure severe trials peacefully is one of the evidences of the power of God at work in our lives.

My body appeared to be showing signs of weakness. Would I experience God's strength in my body's weakness? If God's track record was any indication, then he'd see me through.

The Wisdom of the Ages

The night I had shared my battle weariness (including the possibility of having cancer) with my small group of women (six resident assistants and me), a memory slowly floated into my consciousness as I lay in bed. I remembered that around age twelve, in those adolescent days of reading the Bible for several hours a day, I had asked God to give me wisdom. I figured that if Solomon asked for wisdom, I could ask for wisdom too. Maybe God in his mercy would grant me wisdom.

Back then, I thought my prayer had gone unanswered—sort of like when I had stood in the field with my brother and sister and had waited for God to appear. I assumed Solomon had experienced an instantaneous answer to prayer. I thought he had prayed and, just like that, had become a fount of wisdom. I thought it was "easy peasy," as my daughter Iliana likes to say. I waited a little bit but didn't sense I knew any more after my prayer than before. I had no instantaneous sensation of being wiser. Years later, while remembering that prayer for wisdom, I started to think that maybe God had answered, though not in the way I had anticipated. This is how he answered: God used my desert experiences (suffering) to cultivate his wisdom and power within me.

Wisdom and power are the fruits of God's grace combined with our submissive obedience to God. We all need wisdom to know how to live and how to love one another. We also need the power to put that love into practice. And so it may take the desert to transform us from incorrigible, stubborn, unloving people into wise and submissive daughters and sons of God. That's why the writer of Hebrews tells us:

> During the days of Jesus' life on earth, he offered up prayers and petitions with fervent cries and tears to the one who could save him from death, and he was heard because of his reverent submission. Son though he was, he learned obedience from what he suffered and, once made perfect, he became the source of eternal salvation for all who obey him. (5:7–9)

Jesus had to learn to become weak. We, however, are naturally weak and dependent; we don't need to learn to become weak. We do need to learn to admit our weaknesses and, like Jesus, learn obedience through what we suffer. Again, that doesn't mean we welcome suffering with glee or that we inflict suffering upon others and ourselves in order to teach lessons. But it does mean that God can redeem the most excruciating experiences of our lives as we apply the lessons we learn in our suffering.

From Unwise to Wise

After Peter and John created a public disturbance by healing a lame beggar at the gate called Beautiful, they found themselves in jail, held for questioning by a coterie of everybody who was anybody among the Jewish leaders and intellectuals (Acts 3–4). "By what power or by what name did you do this?" the leaders demanded (4:7). These very important people who had studied and parsed the Scriptures for years, who had been to the best schools, and who thought themselves wise in the ways of God and the world had trouble believing that Yahweh was empowering these backwoods apostles. If anyone had the corner on the God market, the leaders did.

After Peter answered them by saying that he and John had healed the lame man in the name of the resurrected Jesus, the Jesus whom the elite had crucified, these religiously erudite people were stunned. They were shocked by both the courage Peter and John displayed and the facility with which the apostles handled the Scriptures. Luke tells us, "When they saw the courage of Peter and John and realized that they were unschooled, ordinary men, they were astonished and they took note that these men had been with Jesus" (Acts 4:13).

This story reminds us that the wisdom and power of God are available to those of us who spend time with Jesus and apply what he says. This is especially good news for those of us of humble means and origins—the weak ones of this world. Thankfully, God's power and wisdom aren't confined to the halls of elite academic institutions or posh boardrooms. We may never set foot on an Ivy League campus, walk the halls of power, rule from a palace, assert ourselves in a board meeting, hold a leadership position, strike it rich, or become a celebrity—all symbols of this world's knowledge and power structures.

We do well to remember that God reverses the power structures of this world. He casts his lot with those who in their weaknesses admit that they need him. These are the powerful ones. These are the ones God is for and so no one can be against. Theologian Miroslav Volf writes, "The Holy One of Israel, the God of Jesus Christ is on the side of the downtrodden and poor, a God who listens to the cries of the powerless."[3] Especially in the early centuries, those from every strata of society, including rulers and others in authority, would make pilgrimages into the desert in order to receive words of wisdom and spiritual direction from the desert fathers and mothers. It may come as a surprise, but the fact is that most of the desert fathers and mothers were illiterate. They were unschooled. Yet the lives of these desert saints were so powerful that even the powerful in this world braved harsh desert conditions to meet with them.

We see this same situation in the Gospels when Jesus, speaking about John the Baptist, asks the crowd, "What did you go out into the wilderness to see? A reed swayed by the wind? . . . A man dressed in fine clothes? No, those who wear expensive clothes and indulge in luxury are in palaces" (Luke 7:24–25). Jesus knew they wouldn't make the difficult trip into the desert simply to see a well-dressed VIP. Jesus continues, "But what did you go out to see? A prophet? Yes, I tell you, and more than a prophet. . . . I tell you, among those born of women there is no one greater than John; yet the one who is least in the kingdom of God is greater than he" (vv. 26, 28). John's wisdom from above made him so powerful that even the rulers journeyed into the desert to see him. Herod too feared him (and later murdered him only to save face with those at a party [Matt. 14:1–12]).

This phenomenon of disciples making pilgrimages to obtain wisdom from those who've been formed into the image of Christ through suffering isn't just ancient history. One of the wisest and most powerful witnesses of God's ways in recent memory was Mother Teresa. Countless people flocked to the city of Calcutta to receive a word of wisdom from her and to work alongside her and the Sisters of Charity. Throughout the world, even non-Catholics and non-Christians regarded her as a holy woman who was intimate with God. They desired to drink from the fount of her wisdom, for here was a quiet, simple, unassuming woman who submitted herself to God and gained wisdom born of suffering. Mother Teresa has bequeathed to us a treasure trove of wisdom such as, "Do not think that love in order to be genuine has to be extraordinary. What we need is to love without getting tired. Be faithful in small things because it is in them that your strength lies."[4]

There is a wisdom and a power we can gain nowhere else except in our experiences of brokenness in which we submit ourselves to God. Submitting ourselves to God also entails considering the wisdom of those wiser than us. True wisdom begins with our awe of God. This fear of God leads us to trust that he will bring forth wisdom from our God-redeemed brokenness.

Wielding Our Power

"Not many of you should become teachers," the apostle James tells us (James 3:1). The reason, he says, is that God will judge us more strictly—especially our speech. Christian teachers and those who seek to be teachers of the Jesus way have an extra burden of responsibility. I wish more of us who find ourselves in positions of influence would take James seriously.

Some of us desire to be in charge, to lord it over others. While we might not verbally articulate our desires, we choose to climb the ladders of power and success we find in our Christian environments. I've had more than one person tell me they joined a group or committee in order to situate themselves to attain positions of power. The problem is that some of us seek positions of power without having wisdom—including the wisdom to know how to use our power in God-honoring ways. Furthermore, seeking power is not to be our primary motivation. Having power without the wisdom to use it proves disastrous.

In his reflections on the temptations of Jesus, Henri Nouwen has this to say about the temptation of power: "The temptation to consider power an apt instrument for the proclamation of the Gospel is the greatest of all. We keep hearing from others, as well as saying to ourselves, that having power—provided that it is used in the service of God and your fellow human beings—is a good thing."[5]

Nouwen is convinced that this rationalization is what led to the crusades, inquisitions, over-the-top and astronomically expensive cathedrals, and all sorts of other "manipulations." He continues, "Every time we see a major crisis in the history of the church . . . we always see that a major cause of rupture is the power exercised by those who claim to be followers of the poor and powerless Jesus."[6] When we take up the arms of power to get our way, even unwittingly, we work against God's purposes. And here is where Nouwen, someone I consider a modern-day church father, nails it: "What makes the temptation of power so seemingly irresistible? Maybe it is that power offers an easy substitute for the hard task of love. It seems easier to be God than to love God, easier to control people than to love people, easier to own life than to love life. . . . We have been tempted to replace love with power."[7]

It is easier to overpower and control people than to love them. Loving requires death to ourselves and submission to the power of the Holy Spirit. Overpowering and controlling people require reliance on ourselves instead of on God. Nouwen tells us that Jesus faced this temptation his entire life. It is a temptation we too face. What's the solution? It is a willingness to be led.

This temptation isn't limited to those in official ministry positions. God cares about how each of us uses our power and influence. We are mistaken if we think we have none. All of us have a measure of power and spheres of influence. Even Jesus had to learn to rightly use his power on earth. Prior to his incarnation, he knew when and how to use his power. But when he became a human being, born of his mother's womb, he humbled himself. He came to earth as a powerless, vulnerable baby. He had to learn anew how to wisely use his power as the God-man.

In the New Testament, we see that Jesus used his power with restraint. He didn't speed up the natural processes of growth so that he exited the womb one day and was a grown man the next. As a baby, he didn't send the army of heaven to attack Herod and all those who killed the baby boys in an unsuccessful but deadly effort to wipe out his existence. He didn't call fire down from heaven to consume the Roman soldiers who harassed him and his people. On a lighter note, he didn't make all the animals in his vicinity talk in order to entertain children. He didn't cause chocolate candy to rain down from the sky. As far as I know, he didn't do any of that. He limited his supernatural displays of power.

Maybe that's why he hesitated when his mother sidled up to him during the wedding feast at Cana and whispered, "They have no more wine" (John 2:3). By then, she evidently had every reason to believe he had miraculous powers and could do something about the empty wine jars. At first, Jesus wasn't so sure that he should use his power on this occasion. That is why he said, "Woman, why do you involve me? . . . My hour has not yet come" (John 2:4). Part of growing in wisdom and stature meant that Jesus had to learn when and how to use his power. He certainly didn't want to use his power in illegitimate ways. In the case of the wedding feast at Cana, some might say it was a gratuitous use of power. Maybe that's how God's love is—gratuitous. I say that Jesus doesn't shy away from using his power to give us every good and perfect gift. Sometimes a good and perfect gift comes in the form of wine at a wedding—compliments of the power of God.

If Jesus needed wisdom to learn how to use his power, so do we. If the devil tempted Jesus to abuse his power by using it in illegitimate ways, the devil will also tempt us to abuse our power. We need to examine how we, and those in our churches and Christian organizations, use power. We allow horror in the world by allowing power-hungry people to usurp power and also misuse power.

People who don't know how to use power are malodorous to both believers and unbelievers. Perhaps some of us do not speak up about their wrongdoing because we fear what they or others might do to us. We fear loss of reputation or even loss of income. God forbid we find ourselves culpable for their continued wrongdoing and harm of others because we failed to speak up.

Who Are the Mighty Ones among Us?

The wise and powerful come in every shape and size and gender and age. The apostle James tells us how we can spy the wise and powerful among us. We can spot them by their good lives and their "deeds done in a humility that comes from wisdom" (James 3:13). Those whose habitual postures are to lord it over others or who are characterized by arrogance and self-aggrandizing (even in secret) are not the wise and the powerful in the kingdom of heaven. James goes on to tell us: "But if you harbor bitter envy and selfish ambition in your hearts, do not boast about it or deny the truth. Such 'wisdom' does not come down from heaven but is earthly, unspiritual, demonic. For where you have envy and selfish ambition, there you find disorder and every evil practice" (vv. 14–16).

Envy and selfish ambition are unspiritual and demonic and have no place in us or in the body of Christ. We must continually examine ourselves and allow those we trust to tell us the truth in order to make sure these sins haven't infected us while masquerading as wisdom. As James emphasizes, we can identify the wisdom of God in others and in our churches and organizations because it is "pure; then peace-loving, considerate, submissive, full of mercy and good fruit, impartial and sincere" (v. 17).

As I look at that list, I realize I am woefully unwise. I have much to learn about wisdom and humility. I can only imagine that this means more suffering for me. I do not seek to make light of suffering. I'd never want to glorify desert experiences; they come at the expense of comfort and with many tears. All I can conclude is that these experiences are often the ways and means by which God infuses us with wisdom and power. When we surrender our suffering and brokenness to God, we are on the path to wisdom and might.

Several months after my biopsy, we learned that I did not have cancer. However, I was told that, in order to keep an eye on the nodules on my thyroid, I would have to get a checkup every six to twelve months. Because I have already surrendered the outcome of this diagnosis to God's will, I find that I don't worry about the possibility of cancer, but the checkups regularly remind me that my power does not come from my physical health and strength.

11

trembling in fear
and adoration

We exit our wilderness experiences and enter the Promised
Land fearing and trembling and thanking and adoring God
for life. Following a wilderness experience it is hard to take
life for granted.

Marlena Graves

Should We Be Afraid of God?

We three kids were sitting in the backseat of the Ford LTD on
our way to Freeport, the local beach on Lake Erie. My thighs
were sweaty and sticking to the seat, and the open windows did
little to alleviate the sauna-like conditions. Kenny, Michelle, and
I were looking forward to wading in the water, collecting tiny
seashells, and poking around in the sand with whatever sticks we
could find while Uncle Craig stood on the shore chain-smoking.

In the rearview mirror, I could see Uncle Craig's avocado green eyes fix their gaze on me. His was a handsome face. "Fear the Lord, Marlena. Fear the Lord." That was today's injunction. Uncle Craig, one of the gentlest souls on earth, was always telling me about the Lord. He (along with my *abuelita*) was God's mouthpiece to me in those early years. He bought me my first Bible—a children's Bible with a pasty-white little shepherd boy and sheep on the cover.

In the summer of 1988, my family was staying with my paternal grandparents until we could find a place to live. Uncle Craig lived there, as did Uncle Larry from time to time. Most days, Uncle Craig alternated between lying on the couch staring at the ceiling and chain-smoking in the garage. I wondered why he was always tired and how it was possible for him not to be bored. I didn't question it too much; his normal became normal. I've never known him to be any other way.

Every now and then, good-natured Uncle Craig played records or eight tracks for us. He sang along in his crisp baritone voice and encouraged us to sing along too. "Now altogether," he'd say. We'd chime in, "All the leaves are brown, and the sky is gray." That's how I learned some of my favorites songs, like the Mamas and the Papas' "California Dreamin'" and Elvis's "Return to Sender." Once Uncle Craig confided that he composed a song and sent it to Johnny Cash in hopes of hearing it on the radio. He sang it for us: "One night as I walked along this old mission ground, this padre came to me and said, 'Son, change your ways in life.' I said, 'I didn't care no more, I didn't care at all, for my wife left me for another man, another man you see.'" I can still hear the tune in my head.

When I asked my mom about Uncle Craig, she told me he had been in a car accident one rainy night as a result of someone secretly drugging his drink at a party just after high school graduation. Prior to that, Uncle Craig had been a good basketball player with a promising future. The veracity of the story is suspect, but that is what I've always been told.

My precious Uncle Craig, to whom something happened to make his mind less than whole, is the one who tipped me off to the need to live a God-fearing life. Over the years, I thought about what he said and tried to will myself into being scared of God, the same way I forced myself to drink milk and like it. But I just couldn't. "Why am I supposed to be afraid of God?" I asked Uncle Craig. Whatever his response was, it didn't satisfy me. And whatever Uncle Craig meant by "fear God," I had a hunch it didn't mean I should be afraid of God the way I was scared spitless by the only horror movie I accidently laid eyes on when I was four years old.

The neighbors three doors down were the first on the block to own a VCR, and they promptly designated their house the local movie theater. One afternoon, they set up about thirty folding chairs in their living room to accommodate moviegoers. For a small fee, they said, I could see *Strawberry Shortcake*. I sat in the front row next to Jenny, their little girl, while a bunch of rowdy teenagers, including my older brother, sat in anticipation. What I didn't know was that before I could see *Strawberry Shortcake*, I had to sit through *Friday the 13th*. At four years of age in 1982, I had no clue such darkness existed. I kept my eyes glued shut as much as possible. A few times, though, I peeked through the slits in my fingers. Funny how I remember the few seconds of evil I viewed and nothing whatsoever of *Strawberry Shortcake*.

For years I scratched my head trying to figure out what it meant to "fear the Lord." A day or two after the 2004 Indian Ocean tsunami (widely believed to be the most destructive tsunami in history), I was watching news footage about the natural disaster. The television camera panned to the placidly beautiful ocean. Then it panned in the opposite direction, showing a beach littered with dead bodies and debris. According to estimates, the killer wave affected eleven countries and left 150,000 people dead or missing and millions homeless, all in one day.[1] I was stupefied by the contrast between the now peaceful ocean and the life-eating monster it had been only a few days earlier. The dead bodies and debris were evidence of its indiscriminate appetite for destruction. I cried for those whose loved ones the ocean had so mercilessly sent to their watery graves.

Earlier that spring, Shawn and I had taken a trip to Puerto Rico to visit some of my extended family and so that Shawn could have a small taste of the island life I had experienced as a little girl. For a few days, we stayed on Vieques Island, just off the main island, where lots of Puerto Ricans go on vacation. I remember climbing onto a rock that jutted out into the sea. I sat there reading my Bible, journaling, and praying, while just a few feet below me the waves crashed against the rock. After the tsunami, I realized that one freak wave rising out of the calm water could've swallowed me whole. Following the Asian tsunami, I couldn't bring myself to go to the ocean for a long time. I became afraid of the ocean I loved. The reality that the ocean is both beautiful and deadly was too much for me.

The tsunami helped me better understand what it means to fear God. Think of those who refuse to take shelter no matter how many times the authorities tell them to evacuate. They say, "I've lived here thirty years and ridden out lots of storms. I'll be fine." In their overfamiliarity, they assume they'll remain unscathed. We cannot become overly familiar with the holy, just as we cannot become overly familiar with the ocean.

As with the ocean, we cannot bring God under our control. We may unwittingly seek to control him with our obedience and devotion. We think, "God, I've obeyed you. I've been faithful. You owe me one." Or we try to domesticate God with our theologies and explanations and understandings. We forget that none of our theologies completely encapsulate his being and his ways.

For example, we know that Jesus is the Christ and that he is the way, the truth, and the life, but can we ever fully understand all that being the way, the truth, and the life entails? Paul says we cannot, at least not in this life. "For now we see only a reflection as in a mirror; then we shall see face to face. Now I know in part; then I shall know fully, even as I am fully known" (1 Cor. 13:12). God is not an idol that we can tote around and summon whenever we want.

Interestingly enough, the longer we walk with God, the more tempted we are to believe we know more than we actually do. We are in danger of being puffed up with knowledge, tempted to grow careless. "Knowledge puffs up while love builds up. Those who think they know something do not yet know as they ought to know," Paul reminds us (1 Cor. 8:1–2).

The story of the three wise men reveals my need to be humble in my understanding of God. Who were these men? And why did God use astronomy and possibly astrology to announce Christ's birth to these gentile Magi instead of to the leading Jewish scholars of the day? How could first-century, biblically astute memorizers of the law and the prophets miss Jesus? With all their studying and theorizing, they should have been better prepared for Jesus. But when he came, most rejected him. The religious leaders who rejected him considered the cross a curse (and they had good biblical reasons for doing so) and regarded Jesus as a public nuisance and an assault on their religious sensibilities. Not being able to fit God into our own sensibilities or understanding can induce fear in us, just as it did in the biblically literate of the first century. He will do what he will do. He is "I AM WHO I AM" (Exod. 3:14), and that can scare us.

When our daughter Iliana was four years old, we took her canoeing with us. She sat in the middle of the aluminum canoe while Shawn and I lazily paddled. I really wanted her to share in our experience of absorbing the beauty we saw along the river. I wanted her to bask in the glory of God's creation along with us.

However, she would have none of my basking and delighting. Instead, she had several major meltdowns after we started downstream. When she realized she couldn't control the direction of the canoe and had to rely on us to do so, she became woefully out of sorts. If we approached frothing-white rapids or gingerly bumped into the edge of the riverbank, she erupted in hysterics. We spent most of the ride attempting to assure her that the water came only to her waist and that it was normal to bump into the riverbank sometimes. Our assurances failed miserably. Her lack of control and, I suppose, her lack of belief that we were really in control produced tremendous anxiety in her. If we weren't convinced before, that day we learned that our daughter has a deep need for control.

Our daughter isn't the only one who can melt down when a loss of control produces fear. God's refusal to conform to our ways and his refusal to be controlled can send us into hysterics. We have meltdowns because we fear the uncertainty of the unknown. We fear the uncontrollable. And we fear loss—loss that results from surrendering to him. Thomas Aquinas says that we fear the detriment and deprivation of our own good.[2]

Must we be afraid of God, then, as the Israelites were at Mount Sinai (Exod. 19:12), scared that he will hurt us? Need we be children who shrink in fear when approaching our *Abba* Father, worried that he will terrorize us? Jesus does tell us in Matthew 10:28 not to fear human beings who can kill our bodies but instead to fear God, who can destroy both our bodies and our souls in hell. What are we to make of all this?

God doesn't change or suddenly turn on us without warning. He doesn't shower us with love one moment and then abuse us the next. Our Father does not despise us even if, out of ignorance, we are guilty of despising him. He is an unfathomably gracious, loving, and complex being who welcomes us with arms open wide. He longs to embrace us and help us. Like a playful father, he picks us up, delightfully tosses us into the air, catches us, and sets us down on the right path. He never turns on us. It is we who turn away from him.

We should be petrified of turning away from him in an effort to avoid what we fear because doing so means we have chosen our own destruction. Jeremiah 2:19 tells us how terrible it is to turn away from God: "'Your wickedness will punish you; / your backsliding will rebuke you. / Consider then and realize / how evil and bitter it is for you / when you forsake the LORD your God / and have no awe of me,' / declares the Lord, the LORD Almighty."

The Gift of Becoming a Fearless, God-Fearing Person

Fearing God has to do with honoring and respecting him. We constantly think about how we can honor and respect him. He is never an afterthought. We give priority to him and run away from anything that smacks of death, including sin. God and our communion with him are so precious to us that death becomes preferable to hurting or disappointing him. Union with God is what we seek. It is what we hunger for. We willingly make whatever sacrifices are necessary to make him glad and do whatever lies within our power to keep his name from being defamed. Citing Oswald Chambers, we give "our utmost for his highest."[3]

Yes, we fail sometimes. We fall. But we don't want to. Because we are human and because sin and the residue of sin remain, we do what we don't want to do. Overall, though, we are moving forward. We've put our hands to the plough, refusing to look back. If there are any areas of our lives in which we are comfortable with anything less than his will, we know these are areas in which we are immature and have allowed worldly, ungodly fear to prevail. Because we love God, because we honor him, because we fear him, once we become aware of such an area, we surrender it to God. In surrendering the area wherein we've knowingly or unknowingly held back from him, we become rich toward God. Perhaps we can summarize fearing God as being rich toward God in every possible way. At the same time, knowing that God is rich toward us in every possible way allows us to retain a posture of awe so that we tremble whenever we consider who he is. But the key is really knowing that he is rich toward us in every possible way.

It is impossible to honor and respect someone we don't know or someone about whom we've been misinformed. Unless the proper fear of God is formed in us, we will be stingy toward God and our fellow human beings. Small-mindedness about God makes us stingy toward him and also toward others. Fear, or awe of God, is the portal through which the magnificence of his glory is revealed.

In all this we see that fear of God does not give birth to disillusionment but to wisdom. As our awe of God increases, we grow in wisdom and know that God works right here where we are, doing the supernatural work of making us more like Jesus, and bringing forth his kingdom while making us unafraid of whatever confronts us. Fear of God displaces misplaced fear.

This fearful awe is cultivated within us as we learn about who God is and about his intimate relationship with us. In the wildernesses that occur throughout our lives, we experience the depths of God's care. He uses the wilderness, our God-haunted suffering, to form us into people who continually stand in reverential awe of him. This proper fear of God frees us from whatever form our fear of death takes, for in the end, whatever it is we fear, at its root, it is the fear of death. We might also think about how our fears reveal our idols. Do we fear stepping out in faith or trying something new? Do we fear that our good days are in the past? Maybe we idolize perceived comfort and security or the familiar.

Emerging from the wilderness intact but never the same has a way of turning us into God-fearing people. We emerge awestruck. I can think of so many times in my life when I was convinced it was all over.

As a child and a teenager, a lack of emotional insight and communal resources left me without a fighting chance. I daydreamed about what a life free of constant chaos and instability would look like, but I started to believe that I was fated to live a life of misery.

I held on for dear life to the tree of life, while everything else in my life was swept away by a tsunami of pain. The debris beat and battered me. All throughout those dark and awful days when I hated myself because I was stuck in a cycle of sin—out of weariness and out of a desire to alleviate my pain (albeit through destructive means)—I called on God.

The fact that I made it out alive and slowly became a healthy person who welcomed the non-chaotic rhythms of daily life and experienced a measure of peace left me trembling with fearful love. If God in his goodness could deliver me from myself and from a hell of my own making, he could do anything. I felt like Elisha's servant, Gehazi. God tore the veil from my eyes, showing me angel armies surrounding me, ready to fight for my life. It shall forever remain true: those who call on the name of the Lord shall be saved—even though they don't deserve it. His rescue is never contingent on our deserving it. None of us deserves it, not even those of us who fancy ourselves better than most. Because of our almighty God, I stared death and destruction in the face and made it out alive. I need never fear, for now the love of God circulates in my veins.

The one we fear because we cannot control him loves us and ever wills our good. Though we cannot domesticate him, he can domesticate our wild and out-of-control lives. As we get to know the Triune God, our love for him is being perfected, while his love in us is perfecting us. Any wrong fear of God that we have, such as the fear of punishment, begins to recede. As 1 John 4:18 tells us, "There is no fear in love. But perfect love drives out fear, because fear has to do with punishment. The one who fears is not made perfect in love." In a note to those praying alongside her, my friend Judy Douglass described how she was gaining freedom in a situation that had induced recurring fear in her life:

> If I keep love within, I will keep fear without. Which is exactly what the apostle John told us. . . . Instead of remembering the pain of the past, I can remember the love poured over me lavishly, repeatedly, extravagantly by my Father in heaven, by the Son who died for me, by the Spirit who lives in me. Then I can keep love within and fear without. And when fear is out, it is amazing how much more easily I let go.[4]

In Jesus Christ, we are the children of God, and our God will move heaven and earth for us. The knowledge that God deeply loves and cherishes us and will not harm us will slowly begin to siphon off the fear within. We need not fear him or how he'll take care of us. God's love displaces fear.

Being in the kingdom of God ultimately gives us the confidence to live this life as fearless, God-fearing children. Henri Nouwen reminds us that "the house of the Lord is the house of love for all people. There is a circle of safety, intimacy, and hospitality in the house of love. In that house we can slowly let go of our fear and learn to love."[5] Hanging on to fear will keep us from loving and being loved. Fear will take our lives. That is why all throughout the Bible we read, "Be not afraid." Thankfully, our fear-inspiring God is one to whom we can safely surrender all that produces fear in us. We learn to surrender our fears as we live and love among others practiced in releasing their fears. It bears repeating: in God we are as safe as we can be.

God will attend to us in whatever fearful situations we find ourselves. When we sense fear stalking us, no matter what form it takes, when we worry that it will assail us and drown us, we remember God. If we have trouble conjuring up memories of God, we find someone who can remember God for us and with us. God uses Scripture, our prayers, our practice of spiritual disciplines, friends, books, music, and art (among others things) to serve as lifeguards when we are drowning in fear. Regarding the use of memory to combat fear, Jo Kadlecek writes, "Maybe that is why pastors or priests suggest fear is a spiritual memory lapse, a case of forgetting God loves a human's soul enough to protect her."[6]

If we drown, going down to our death (whether physical or another death of self) will be a drowning in God's ocean of love, from which we will be raised. His currents will take us where we belong. The currents of his love do not discard us like a forgotten pile of debris. "To pause at the shore of mystery," Kadlecek says, "is to hold your fears up against its magnitude. Its enormity alone reminds a soul that she is small. . . . And that recognition is strangely soothing."[7]

Irresistible Adoration

I used to run before the podiatrist told me I should stop running. Growing up, I had pain in my legs, knees, ankles, and feet whenever I'd stand too long or do the kinds of exercise that are hard on the shins. I never had these pains checked out because we didn't have the money to see a doctor for non-life-threatening illnesses. As a twentysomething, I found out I had flat feet. Finally, an explanation! My flat feet are the reason I have great affection for Psalm 18:36: "You provide a broad path for my feet, so that my ankles do not give way."

It was on a run, shortly after my high school deliverance, that I slowed down to a walk. My knees and ankles hurt, but my soul throbbed with the fullness of the love of God. I was bursting with adoration. His recent against-all-odds rescue and deliverance had refreshed and invigorated me. He had snatched me from the enemy's watering mouth even though I had offered myself to him by offering myself to someone to whom I didn't belong. It wouldn't be the last time I'd revel in God's penchant for coming through.

We must be careful to whom and to what we offer ourselves. Much suffering occurs when we offer ourselves to people, circumstances, and ideas to whom we don't belong and refuse those to whom we do belong. We cannot offer up our souls and expect to be all right.

As I walked, adoration saturated my insides. I racked my brain for the loftiest words and expressions I could find to express the praise and thanksgiving surging within. I quickly became disgusted by my lack of facility with the English language. I knew words existed that could better give voice to what I was experiencing, to express the depths of adoration inside me. But I couldn't find them.

It was an attempt to name that which cannot be named. Eventually, I gave up. Better to join the angels who have never stopped declaring, "Holy, holy, holy is the Lord God Almighty, who was, and is, and is to come" (Rev. 4:8). I latched on to murmuring "Holy, holy, holy . . ." as I rounded the bend on my walk home. There on Mystic Park Road, along Oil Creek, I began wondering how, with robust reverence, these creatures endlessly cry, "Holy, holy, holy is the Lord God Almighty, who was, and is, and is to come." How do they continue throughout eternity without tiring?

Not even the red-bearded fellow twice my age who slowed down in his muffler-dragging, old beater to catcall could interrupt my reverie. I ignored him. He sped away. Now I understood how the angels could continue their adoration throughout eternity: adoration continually surges through these angelic creatures who flank the throne of God. It isn't work for them; there is nothing laborious about it. They are simply and gladly vocalizing the endless stream of praise that flows through them. They cannot help but repeat, "Holy, holy, holy is the Lord God Almighty."

At first, we feel as though our wilderness experiences are suffocating us and killing us. But our God-bathed wilderness experiences have two results: the opening of our eyes and the unclogging of the pores of our souls. A God-bathed wilderness experience is a cleansing experience. We exit refreshed, fearing, and praising. Every part of us—mind, spirit, and body—cries out in praise and thanksgiving. Irresistible adoration.

How sacred and holy is this life. Every day, at work or at play, in sickness and in health, in suffering and in delight, in the mundane and in the exhilarating, God is communicating with us. He is voicing the beauty of what it means to belong to him and what it means for us to be in him and he in us. He is parading before us and in us the beauty of his delight. Our good Father continually invites us to share in the self-giving love experienced by the three members of the Trinity, a love that spills into all creation and into us. We must choose to accept the invitation to marinate in the love of God. As Father Greg Boyle writes while quoting Ignatius of Loyola:

> Jesus chose to marinate in the God who is always greater than our tiny conception, the God who "loves without measure and without regret."

To anchor yourself in this, to keep always before your eyes this God is to choose to be intoxicated, marinated in the fullness of God.[8]

I find myself tearing up a lot and not just because of all the suffering in the world. I think these tears are a gift, proof that the wilderness has tenderized my soul. Whether my tears are due to awe-inspired adoration, continued marvel at the goodness and beauty of God, or soul-shaking laughter, they come as I fearfully and wonderfully participate in God's life. (Uncle Craig, thank you for starting me off on this journey. I think I am starting to internalize what it means to fear and adore God.)

I think there's a mixture of tears and laughter-type adoration because I finally have a life, and I can see life in others and in the world. I am intoxicated with life, marinating in the full life of God. When we are full of the life of God, those who don't understand may think us drunken fools, like those at the first Pentecost, or clowns of God, like St. Francis of Assisi. Somewhere it has been said that St. Francis stood on his head so he could see the world aright.

The gifts of fear and adoration will lead us to do things, to live life with abandon, because we know in whom we live and move and have our being. Upon spotting Jesus wherever he happens to show up, we just might throw our arms around him, hold on to him tightly, plant kisses on his face, and then crumple into a heap of adoration as we wet his feet with our tears and bathe his feet with the perfume of a broken and poured out life. What a greeting!

We may even find ourselves dancing naked before God as David did. In our case, naked probably means being wholly vulnerable before God and trusted others, for we have nothing to hide. Yes, we may be surprised to find ourselves dancing and laughing and leaping with all our might because of the joyful adoration that is eager to escape us. These are expressions of fearful adoration. Expressions of joy. And they are all right. Acceptable and pleasing to God. God doesn't mind if we dance a jig of adoration. He takes delight in our expressions of fearful adoration, gifts bestowed to us in abundance as we exit the wilderness.

12

children in the kingdom of God

> For we have sinned and grown old and our Father is younger than we.
>
> G. K. Chesterton

A gift: each with-God wilderness experience makes us younger and more childlike. I am growing younger every day, my life less complex. I am like a young child who springs up at the crack of dawn, long before anyone else is awake, and eagerly snatches open the curtains to behold a world teeming with life. I am being trained to turn my gaze on life, on the good, and so I am becoming like that which I behold. Oh, I do not deny there is death, only now I understand what my Father has been saying all along: that death holds no power over me. I do not need to be scared. Life conquers death, as Aleksandr Solzhenitsyn has said.[1]

In order to enter into all that the kingdom of God has for us, we must become little children—little children who clamber all over Jesus.

In my own life, corruption and adult concerns entered into my psyche too early, eclipsing any experience of an age of innocence. I had to leave childish things behind before I even had the chance to be childish. But God rescued me from the far-off country and, like Jonah, redeposited me into the kingdom of light, into the kingdom of the Son he loves. It was then that I started learning how to live as a free person and not as a slave to my emotions and desires. God gave me an identity. When I was nineteen years of age, just a few days shy of my twentieth birthday, God spectacularly rescued me from myself, and I had the sense that I was being reborn.

I now know that in some sense we are called to be born again every day. We are to leave our thoughts and our ways of doing things behind and be reborn to God's ways of doing things. Being reborn is painful. Going through the birth canal is always painful. That is why U2 sings, "Yahweh, Yahweh, always pain before a child is born." But rebirth into new ways of being is more difficult if we resist, if we cling to what was.

Emerging from a severe depression, which lasted throughout my freshman and sophomore years of college, was part of my rebirth. Or should I call it "resurrection"? The depression was due to my death-filled decisions as a teenager, lack of money for school, and internalized anger and unforgiveness I harbored toward my parents and myself.

As a young child in the kingdom, I had all sorts of questions for Jesus. To begin with, "What was I supposed to do now?" I had forsaken the habits of sin and death. I certainly didn't want to have traversed my first great wilderness and have had my soul swept clean of demons just to have them come back and vengefully take up residence in force, seven times stronger and more determined to stay than before. I knew this to be a real possibility from having read Scripture and having heard stories of others who had, in a way, repented of their repentance. As I sat in Jesus's lap for a while, spending time with God in a myriad of ways, I learned a few things about being a child in his kingdom, about what I was supposed to do and not do, and about who I was supposed to be.

Rest

My twenty-year-old soul felt tired and haggard. I'd been in the war zone for so long that I didn't know any other kind of life. I was always on watch, on guard for the next onslaught. For the first time, I felt safe enough to rest. God continued to reassure me that he would be awake during the night watches; there was no need for me to stay up. He was on duty and was competent enough to care for me and protect me. "In peace I will lie down and sleep, / for you alone, LORD, / make me dwell in safety" (Ps. 4:8). I didn't have to weary myself with trying to figure things out anymore. I didn't need to worry about how I'd manage to come up with the money to make it through college or about if and when I'd get married. What I needed to do was leave the figuring out of things to the parent, to our heavenly Father. "Go to bed, Marlena, go to bed," I sensed him urging. God's children need their rest so they can grow. In resting from worry, we grow up in God.

The Lord assured me that he'd gently nudge me on the shoulder when it was time for me to rise and act. It would be then, not before, that I would need to move from an obediently restful posture to an actively obedient posture. Being well rested would allow me to behave in peace and not become frantic at the onset of stress. I am responsible for waking when he nudges me and for obeying once he gives me an assignment. These are simple truths. Yet it's the simple and obvious truths that we often make complex and have trouble obeying.

Our Father, who knows us well, has allowed us to be in this place, this place where we are right now.[2] We may not remain right here, but here is where God has allowed us to be in this moment. And he has given us everything we need to live in the present moment. It is here that we must nestle into his bosom and, if need be, fall asleep—all while resting in his goodness. His presence is a place of restful delight. He will put us down to run and play when the time comes.

As a parent, I watch my little girls sleep. Watching them moves me to think about the expression "sleeping like a baby." The phrase conjures up images of carefree and restful sleep. I know God wants me to sleep like a baby. He wants me to know that he is working and planning for my good while I sleep. It would be very sad if my own girls, "the ladies" as we are sometimes inclined to call them, stayed up all night worrying about how they'd manage the wherewithal to live. Their staying up would indicate a deficiency in trust, that they didn't feel safe and secure in my love. I hope they never arrive at a point where they remain awake with worry.

Not long ago, I stayed at the Jesuit Retreat House in Parma, Ohio, one of the Cleveland suburbs. At our orientation, Sister Mary Ann told us it was the first retreat house in the United States. I was happy to be there and ready to embrace whatever God had for me. Shawn graciously, as always, agreed to watch the girls for five days so I could rest and write. Little Valentina was teething and waking frequently at night. He'd see her through the night so I could have the opportunity to experience uninterrupted sleep and to rejuvenate.

The first night I didn't sleep as well as I wanted. It wasn't because I was worried or wound up. I chalked it up to sleeping in a new bed and to the sounds that came from the exposed pipes that hung low from the ceiling in my room. Around midnight, I heard thumping. "Is that the plumbing making noises because someone is showering, or is someone knocking on my window because they've been locked out?" I wondered.

I lay in bed quiet as a mouse, trying to decide what to do. If the banging continued, it must be someone wanting to be let in. If it subsided, it was the pipes. Right about the time I was considering getting out of bed to peek through the blinds, it stopped.

When it was all said and done, I went to sleep way past midnight. (I didn't look at the clock for fear of becoming discouraged by the late hour.) I dozed off only to be awakened by sunshine streaming through the blinds. I stayed in bed hoping to fall back to sleep. I didn't. I looked at the clock and saw it was a few minutes after six. "No use staying in bed. Maybe I should take an early morning walk on the prayer path," I thought. I got dressed and started off with vigor.

I would attack my walk and attack the day, get some blood pumping through my veins, try to walk off some of the post-pregnancy pounds that were clinging to me. I was rounding the first bend, not a hundred feet from the retreat house, when on my left something started. A doe sprang to her feet and stared at me with her big, brown eyes. I stared back, captivated. I stepped back, not wanting to move forward for fear of scaring her away. As my eyes adjusted to my surroundings, I noticed five other deer peacefully nestled among the bed of leaves on the forest floor. If not for the doe that had started, I wouldn't have seen them—they blended in so well with the surroundings. After a minute, she bent her legs and slowly settled into her spot on the forest floor. The other deer gave me a casual glance as they continued lounging. She, however, continued to stare. I walked back to the bench I had just passed and sat down.

I thought about that beautiful doe, wishing we could be friends. I wondered what she was thinking. I imagined her having thoughts like, "What is that two-legged thing doing?" I decided not to continue my walk but to stay and listen for what God might be telling me among the deer. It was a simple but beautifully profound picture of what he had been trying to communicate over the last year: "Nestle in me, like the deer nestling in the leaves on the forest floor in the early dawn. Peacefully rest in my care. I will always take care of you."

The picture of the resting deer serves as an image of rest that I routinely bring before my mind's eye. While I've started to learn how to rest in God, rest is a gift I continually need to learn how to receive. Whether due to life transitions or new trials and tribulations, I am still tempted to stay awake and active in order to manage life when I should be resting. Here Gregory of Nyssa's words about the Lord's Prayer are a helpful reminder: "Our Lord tells us to pray for today, and so he prevents us from tormenting ourselves about tomorrow."[3] I know I am learning to rest because I rarely torment myself about tomorrow anymore. It is a communion-with-God wilderness gift.

Once we discover what it takes for us to rest well and how we best rejuvenate, we can begin to find rest in the various circumstances in which we find ourselves. If we can learn to rest in the most tumultuous wilderness environs, we can rest in the rigmarole of everyday life. We need intervals of rest every day. Rest is an integral part of our daily rhythms. We shouldn't balk at asking others to help us in our pursuit of much-needed rest. I think of mothers and fathers (and other caregivers) of young children. I think of those who are caring for aging or debilitated parents. They shouldn't hesitate to ask others for help so they can rest. And we should not hesitate to offer our help to them and others who need rest. God gives us the gift of rest, and we can give it to others. God gently and persistently reminds us of his gift to us, the gift of nestling into his arms and sleeping like a baby or like a deer on the forest floor at the break of dawn. He gives us the gift of childhood rest. Will we receive his gift?

Play

Not only do we leave the wilderness with a greater ability to rest like a sleeping baby who is cradled in the arms of God, but we also become more playful. I am growing younger because the fear and anxieties that were weighing me down, those elements that were wrinkling and withering my soul, are dissipating. Every wilderness experience strips me of layers of these soul-withering elements. Consequently, I am becoming a tender shoot even as my years slowly ebb away. This is how eternal life affects us. Knowing God through Jesus Christ his Son grows us younger. We become children in the kingdom. And if we know one thing about healthy children it's this: they love to play.

After I emerged from that protracted wilderness experience that lasted most of my freshman and sophomore years of college, I sensed God not only giving me permission but also encouraging me to play—and to play often. Playing is an expression of joy. Everyday joy. Exiting the wilderness, we are overjoyed because we know what it is like to stare death (in its myriad forms) right in the face, and yet we've survived. It's not mere survival, a barely alive or barely getting by survival. It's a thriving survival; it's the life that God is known for producing in us. It may come slowly, but it comes. Just when we thought it was all over for us, when we thought we would certainly perish, God came. He came and rescued us, reminding us that he is as faithful as ever, which is always.

It's not that we forget or dismiss the pain and suffering that we or others have been through; we see and experience pain and suffering for what they are. It's that we now know pain and suffering are not all there is to the world. Our wilderness experiences have opened up new channels within our souls so that we have a greater capacity for life. We're able to see reality more clearly. After so much grief and pain and near hopeless-ness, we are fresh with life—playful. Not overly sober. Play is an expression of our celebration.

And yet as a twenty-year-old, I didn't know how to play. I didn't know how to have fun. I had been much too serious for too long. There were moments of levity in my life, but they were few and far between. I didn't have a hobby as a child; we couldn't afford music or dance or swim lessons. I'd ride my bike every once in a while, throw the blue bouncy ball from the second-story window of our home (the one we moved into after the green trailer) so that either Michelle or Kenny could catch it, and sometimes I'd make snow angels in the winter snow after shoveling the driveway. Yet, my recreation, when not doing chores, consisted mostly of reading and listening to music. I was in my head a lot.

I do remember a time in fifth grade when my siblings and I painted the large, bench-like rocks in the grove of trees near our trailer with some leftover white paint. The little grove of saplings was my sanctuary. I'd cajole Kenny and Michelle into sitting down on the white "pews" while I used one of the rocks as my pulpit and delivered a sermon. That was the extent of my play.

Those days are long gone, never to return. A sense of nostalgia overtakes me when I remember the grove of saplings and the infrequent but simple play with my younger sister and brother. The memories make me wish we all lived side by side and could spend extended periods playing together now as adults—now that I am more playful and carefree.

I never played with dolls and stuffed animals. But now I do. The summer after I met Shawn, I had the inclination to buy him a Beanie Baby. It was a Colobus monkey, significant in that it was a reminder of the playful and eminently endearing Colobus monkeys we had observed at the zoo. Those zoo monkeys reminded us of each other and the playfulness that oozed from us so naturally when we were together. We called the stuffed monkey Mankel. He is a boy. And because it wasn't good that he should be alone, we bought another monkey and named her Mankey. They are brother and sister.

But don't you call either of them a "stuffed animal" in front of us. That'd be sacrilege. They've been alive fifteen years (but are perpetually two years old), the way the Velveteen Rabbit is alive, the way the characters from our favorite books have a vitality about them. We have taken them everywhere with us, even to the beach on our honeymoon. They are a part of us, a part of our family. They have unique and distinct voices, personalities, and affections. In any given situation, Shawn and I could tell you what Mankel and Mankey would do. Mankel is always into mischief, and Mankey is sweet, a lover of the beautiful things in life. But she'll take on the long arm of the law with Mankel or with us if we get out of line. They also play musical instruments. Mankel plays the trombone and the piano, and Mankey plays the flute.

Mankel and Mankey are family treasures. Our girls are not allowed to play with them without supervision, and then only once in a while. These days, Mankel and Mankey stay at home for safekeeping. If anything were to happen to them, we'd be devastated. I used to wonder why some little children were devastated when they lost their special friends. Now I fully understand.

Iliana, our oldest, cracks me up with her creativity and imagination. When she was three, whenever we gave her a little friend (stuffed animal) or a doll that had clothes on, the next morning the clothes of one doll would be on another doll or (in what must have taken considerable effort) on a much larger stuffed animal. As she accumulated more friends and dolls, there was no telling who would be wearing what. Three years later, she still dresses her friends really well. I bust up whenever she puts Barbie clothes on, let's say, little rubber lizards. Around the age of three, she also started stuffing her friends under her pajamas. I wasn't pregnant when she started this, but many of my friends were. Even now, on random evenings when I check in on her, I still find her with Beanie, a cream-colored rabbit, protruding from her belly while she sleeps.

As her parent, I think it's precious. But it's more than that. Whenever I catch her playing alone or with Shawn, or whenever I play with her, a deep satisfaction wells up within me, forcing a smile across my face. My soul satisfaction comes from knowing that she enjoys playing and that she feels the freedom to play; it comes from being able to share with her both play and laughter. My husband Shawn often says, "Laughter is a spiritual discipline. It's a form of subversion. It's a way of upending the perversion of the world. It's a way to delight in goodness." And so I laugh along with her and others. The worries and tragedies of this world haven't robbed her of her childhood.

And they no longer rob me of my childhood. In the wilderness I learned that God is gradually restoring the years that the locust have eaten (see Joel 2:25). I thought my childhood had vanished never to be seen again—devoured by a swarm of locusts in the form of my own sins, the sins of others, and other complications from the fall. And of course, in a very real sense, my childhood did vanish. What I am experiencing now is a resurrection of my childhood. It's a second childhood as I learn what it means to be a trusting child at play in the kingdom of God.

I trust that Valentina, like Iliana, will be able to experience the fullness of childhood. It is my wish not only for my children but for all the children of the world. And it is God's wish for every single one of us. It is my hope that when God makes all things new he will redeem the lost childhoods of the innocents.

God also plays. How exactly and where exactly he is playing all throughout the universe I cannot fully know. Perhaps G. K. Chesterton's observation will be of some help: "A child kicks his legs rhythmically through excess, not absence of life. Because children have abounding vitality, because they are in spirit fierce and free, therefore they want things repeated and unchanged. They always say, 'Do it again'; and the grown up person does it again until he is nearly dead. For grown up people are not strong enough to exult in monotony."[4]

Yet, Chesterton suggests, God is different from those "grown up people":

> But perhaps God is strong enough to exult in monotony. It is possible that God says every morning, "Do it again" to the moon. It may not be automatic necessity that makes all daisies alike; it may be that God makes every daisy separately, but has never got tired of making them. It may be that he has the eternal appetite of infancy; for we have sinned and grown old and our Father is younger than we.[5]

As a child in the kingdom, I am reminded that we live in an enchanted world—a world of delight and a world at play. There are both evil and forces of evil. This I know all too well. But there is also much good. Part of that goodness includes God and his holy angels at play.

I can hear some of the songs God plays in the sound of the wind rustling through the pines, in the sounds the leaves make as they skip and dance and swirl about on a fall day. Perhaps the angels are swirling and twirling with the leaves, twirling about while remaining ever in step with the Trinitarian dance. I believe they are extending an invitation for all of us to join in.

I hear his music in the song of a whale, a song given to her by God and one that she sings back to him in praise. I hear his music in the peck, peck, pecking of a woodpecker and in the songs of the cicadas on a summer's day. I hear the music of God in the choirs of birds who hop around on the tree branches close by. I laugh when they become silent upon noticing my presence. "I see you," I tell them. "I know you are there and that you will start singing once I walk far enough away." Funny birds.

God's playful spirit is evident. Think of the creatures of the deep, the strangeness of their shapes and of their appearances. I see the beautiful colors of fish and of flowers, and I think to myself, "Crayons can only try to imitate the scintillating color palate of creation." God paints the earth and everything in it with a beauty all his own. He is playing as he is painting our lives beautiful too.

I can imagine Jesus arm wrestling with his disciples. I reckon they tumbled and tussled about on their walks from here to there. I sometimes imagine there being a last-days wrestling match with Samson, David and his mighty men, Shawn, Kenny, the disciples, and anyone else who wants to join in. In my mind's eye, I see God's children tumbling about, leaping back into the pile to determine who will be the last man standing. My brother, Kenny, tells me that he sometimes imagines Elijah running ahead of Ahab's chariot. I wonder who would win the footrace on the Lord's field day in those days when all has been made new. Will it be old Elijah full of the strength of a young man or someone alive now?

Oh, the ways we can play and the ways God plays. I can imagine Jesus playing children's games with the children he encountered. And after the resurrection, perhaps he formed a circle hand-in-hand with children and those who have grown young, grown to be children after spending time with him. Maybe in their joy they play a version of ring-around-the-rosy (but without its somber allusion). And maybe they all fall down in stitches of laughter because they are grateful for being alive and together, because the crucifixion didn't have the last word, because the crucifixion wasn't their last memory of Jesus. Together they laugh away sorrow and inhale life. You and I can also have joy because the wilderness teaches us that suffering doesn't have the last word in our lives either. "Christ plays in ten thousand places," Gerard Manley Hopkins wrote.[6] Yes, he does. I believe he does. Can you see him at play in you and in me and in all of creation?

Attentiveness and Curiosity

Children are extremely curious and take note of just about everything.

Children are sponges. For good or for ill, they imitate us. Iliana mimics our vocal intonations, and she has also picked up much of Shawn's vocabulary. It is jarring to hear her use grown-up words in context. On the negative side, she imitates displays of my impatience.

I have observed that the closer I get to God and the more childlike I become, the more I imitate him and the more I notice what he notices. Thankfully, in God there is no darkness at all, no negative qualities to imitate. Today, I am much more curious than in my childhood and teenage years. The wilderness trained me in the powers of observation. I exit the wilderness with sharpened perceptions of life.

God notices the number of hairs on our heads, each sparrow that falls to the ground, and wildflowers growing in fields humans will never see. I mimic him in noticing details of creation. I often look out my window as we are traveling in a car and notice a cat making its way through a field. I wonder about the adventure of that cat, where he or she, this creature of God, is going. Seeing the cat on its way brings me joy, the same way seeing groundhogs grazing along the side of the road brings me joy. I am like a child who notices every creepy crawly thing in the house or on a footpath. Like Iliana, I feel bad for the worms who've been trampled by pedestrians on a sidewalk after a cloudburst. I feel bad about killing ants and other creeping bugs in my house. (Admittedly, spiders, mosquitoes, and flies aren't included in my sympathies for some reason.)

And, of course, I notice the trees in all their majesty. I am particularly drawn to the old, thick ones with massive trunks and branches that spread out. I often wonder what they would tell me if they could speak. They've seen and heard much. They have been around far longer than I have and will remain after I am gone. God likes trees. He made so many of them. And not only do they bequeath us with beauty, but they also give us oxygen and shade and food and shelter.

One thing I admire about Iliana is that she will talk to anyone. She is quite indiscriminate in her love. She is like many other children I have observed, children who find joy in being with others—no matter their ethnicity, ability, or disability. My wilderness experiences have served to make me younger in God, more childlike in the kingdom. Consequently, like Iliana and other young children, I have become more aware of the uniqueness and preciousness of others. People have myriad characteristics that render them lovely in the sight of God and in my sight too. Their beauty speaks to me of his handiwork. My love has grown more indiscriminate, less prejudicial. Wilderness reprioritizes our values so that we prize what's most important. In our wilderness experiences, the knowledge that we all carry in us, vestiges of glory, is deeply ingrained. The holiness of God is in us insofar as his image remains in us.

Beloved

Our Father, who also has the dear qualities of a mother, adores us more than anything. Looking back, I see my wilderness experiences have in the profoundest of ways instilled in me a knowledge of God's adoring love for me and others. This is also true of the God-haunted wilderness experiences of those in Scripture and church history.

God adores us with the same enthusiastic vigor with which Iliana adores Shawn and me. Whenever we are gone for a stint (whether it be for work, shopping, or a conference), when we return, Iliana, with eyes full of dancing delight, runs headlong into us and hugs us as tightly as she can. Shawn quickly sweeps her off her feet, buries his head in her face, and utters, "Daddy missed you." I cannot sweep her off her feet as quickly or as easily as Daddy does. So she buries her head in my chest as I lean over to kiss her, or I slowly lift her up and balance her on my hip. And Iliana isn't the only one filled with delight. Even Valentina's eyes light up when one of us walks into the room. Now she too is at the point where she runs to greet us when we arrive. They are demonstrative in their love for us.

God-haunted wilderness experiences teach us that we are God's beloved, and his adoration for us is incomprehensible. He misses us and wants to be with us even more than we want to be with him. I know this is so because I know how desperately I want to be with my children and in good relationship with them. And I am not the perfect parent our heavenly Father is, perfect in all his ways and perfect in his parenting. As we walk with him, rest in him, and play under his watchful eye, we will catch him gazing at us. Ours is a God who cannot take his eyes off us.

All these things I learned and experienced in the wilderness. The wilderness can be a difficult place, but it's also the place where miracles and epiphanies occur, the place where we come to know and see God.

Zephaniah 3:17 says, "The LORD your God is with you, / the Mighty Warrior who saves. / He will take great delight in you; / in his love he will no longer rebuke you, / but will rejoice over you with singing." In our wilderness comforts and deliverances, we experience God's delight in us, the lullabies of shalom and adoration that he sings over us, his beloved children. And in the same way that Valentina is just now, after months of quiet listening, able to join us enthusiastically in song, soon we begin mouthing songs of praise and adoration back to God. Our lives become a song of adoration to God, a song those about us can hear.

If this is how our Father, who has demonstrated that he will spare no expense for our lives by sacrificing his Son on our behalf, loves us his children, can we not entrust ourselves into his care? When he puts us in the corner or disciplines us because he loves us, can we not trust him? When we have no idea what is going on, when wilderness pain has shattered us and those we love into pieces, we have to draw on our knowledge of how he loves us.

James Bryan Smith advises us to repeat this truth about our identity and life in the kingdom, especially in the midst of difficulty: "I am a child of God, one in whom Christ dwells, and I am living in the unshakable kingdom of God."[7] As a child of God, the riches of our Father's affection are ours. In him we find favor and help in our time of need. Smith tells us that repeating this truth will help us learn it. He is right.

Our Father, our God, will never do us any harm. On the contrary, he will pursue us with goodness and mercy. He does well by his children in this world of sinfulness and pain. However, we may have to redefine what *well* means, because *well* certainly doesn't mean getting everything we want when we want it. It may take us an entire lifetime to learn what *well* is. We might have to rearrange our thought patterns, as journalist and author Jo Kadlecek observes: "There are times when little children must *rearrange* many of their thought patterns previously held, that is, they do if they want to grow. . . . Perhaps part of learning to belong, of discovering our identity, is unearthed in places where we least expect to find it."[8]

That doesn't mean we don't ask God for things because we fear that our definition of *well* and his definition of *well* are different. As God's children, we can be clear and precise with our requests. We don't need to be shy about asking for ourselves or for others. Our daughter Iliana is not shy about making her requests known, whether they are needs or wants. I am not offended when she makes a request. We don't need to waste time beating around the bush with our requests to God either. God is on our side. He is not a parent who says, "No, no, no, no!" incessantly and capriciously.

Let us rehearse this reality as a liturgy for our lives as often as we need to: God has given us everything for our enjoyment and everything we need for life and godliness—not just in heaven but here. And let's remember too that he loves to surprise us with good gifts. He even surprises us with gifts for which we haven't asked. The gift of eternal life in Jesus was his idea long before any of us were born! He is always cooking up schemes for bringing us joy. I heard Dallas Willard once say that joy is a "pervasive sense of well-being." How have we been surprised by joy most recently? It'll do our souls good to contemplate God's goodness to us, his adoration of us, and his enjoyment of us, his infinitely beloved children.

Our God-haunted wilderness experiences serve to help us. Our experiences deepen our adoration of him and cement in us the knowledge that we are deeply adored. And thus, a deep experience of mutual adoration is a wilderness gift of God.

13

a human being fully alive

Blessed is the one who perseveres under trial because, having stood the test, that person will receive the crown of life that the Lord has promised to those who love him.

James 1:12

Life Begets Life

I experience the greatest divine growth spurts deep in the wilderness, in the midst of wild and unwelcomed pain. God uses the suffering I experience in the desert wilderness to show me who I am without him, to drive me to repentance, and to make me holy and wholly alive.

If you've read through this book, you've noticed that I've alluded to one of my favorite verses on several occasions: "The thief comes only to steal and kill and destroy; I have come that they may have life, and have it to the full" (John 10:10). Jesus came that we might have eternal life. What does eternal life mean? According to John 17:3, it means to know Jesus Christ. Growing deeper in our relationship with Jesus and in the knowledge of who he is will result in an increasingly full life here and now and an assurance that we will always be with Christ because we know him. The eternal life that bubbles forth from our lives through our knowing Jesus results in a deeper love for others. And still, we cannot yet know all the implications of eternal life.

One night, I ran outside to move the car off the street and onto the driveway. As I closed the door and looked up, I was smitten by the full moon as it emerged from thick blankets of cloud cover. "I didn't know you were there," I whispered softly. The brightly lit moon with its jovial face was God's gift to me on a crisp summer night that could've been mistaken for mid-autumn. God smiled at me in the sudden appearance of the moon. I reveled in his smile and stared at the moon and thought about the billions of people who have lived on our planet and have looked up at the same moon. I thought about all the animals and insects going about their business under the light of the moon. Our moon and the stars I couldn't see are night-lights God provides to comfort us and remind us of his care in the darkness.

I felt small and insignificant yet at the same time known by God, intimately connected to others, all of us God's cared-for creation. It was one of those nights when I felt myself most awake and alive. I was taken with the knowledge that there is so much more to reality than the slice of life I have known. There is so much more to reality than I will ever know. This reality comes from the infinite life of our God, "who gives life to the dead and calls into existence the things that do not exist," as Paul tells us (Rom. 4:17 NRSV). I know what it is like to be dead and then alive again. It's a feeling of fresh aliveness. I always want to choose life. God has called forth this life out of me by reconciling me to himself. Not only has God called forth life from me, but now I also have the capacity to absorb life. My capacity is growing. In reconciliation, there is abundant life for us and, therefore, for others. God is so generous with life, so very generous.

"All creatures of our God and King, lift up your voice and with us sing. Oh, praise him! Alleluia!" sang my soul.[1] "Let everything that breathes praise the LORD! / Praise the LORD!" (Ps. 150:6 NRSV). All of this life, all of us, and the rest of creation were birthed from trinitarian life. Beautiful God. Beautiful life of God! The gift of life is incomprehensible. Incomprehensible! It is beautiful and holy.

The Desert Blooms

No one can predict exactly when a desert will bloom. And some deserts bloom more regularly than others. Mark Dimmit, director of natural history at the Arizona-Sonora Desert Museum, says that as far as desert blooms go, "the necessary conditions are not precisely known" and "many interacting variables affect the phenomenon."[2] As with the physical desert, so with the spiritual desert. Just as there is life buried under rock-hard desert sands, there are seeds of life buried deep inside us.

If in our wilderness we continue in communion with God and do not turn our backs on him, we will emerge tender from our suffering, nearer to God, and compassionate toward others. We will move closer to union with God—union in purpose and in intimacy. We will also emerge with the capacity to bear more fruit than when we first entered.

God knows what will trigger the desert bloom in us. He can bring about the seasonal rains and precise conditions to trigger a bloom. Our life seeds will germinate in our deserts, and they will flourish in unexpected times and in unexpected places when we leave the desert. Our increasing fruitfulness is a direct result of our time in the desert.

The Gift of Life Comes in Various Forms

In college, I used to ask God about the purpose of my suffering and also the purpose of all the words and ideas in my head. I was always thinking about him and the lessons I was learning. I wondered if my suffering was pointless, if my desert would ever bloom. I desired to share my lessons with others for their encouragement and whatever other possible benefits they might receive, but I didn't see how it would happen.

I didn't think I'd be able to testify effectively to God's goodness in the land of the living because of economic disadvantages and because of being a woman. I never felt bad about being a woman with my gifts and my interests until I attended a Christian college. "Why would you do this to me, God?" I wondered. Why would he form me into a woman with pastoral gifts and sensibilities, a woman with a message, only so that I could be rejected by many, especially by men, because of the vessel in which the message was found? In my college environment, I felt that my gifts were unwelcomed and unwanted. And since my gifts are such an integral part of who I am, I felt personally rejected. I was most unwelcomed and unwanted in the places within the church where I felt most comfortable and where I could best contribute. "It'd be so much easier if I were a man!" I'd often say to myself.

But I would soon learn that my gender, my economic disadvantages, and my past were no barriers to God's work in bringing about life through me. And these things couldn't keep me from *receiving* life either. In his great kingdom reversals, God turns our disadvantages on their heads. It was one of the earliest times I discovered that in my weaknesses (or perceived weaknesses) I was strong, and that God's abundantly fruitful life and living streams of water would issue forth through me no matter what, as long as I was open to God's life in and through Jesus.

The key is whether or not we are open to new life. You'd think we would be, but sometimes we are not. If we are going to be open to God's new life in us, we must be good stewards of our pain. Frederick Buechner tells us that being a good steward of our pain, which includes our disadvantages, "involves being alive to your life."[3] Being alive to life "involves the risk of being open, of reaching out, of keeping in touch with the pain as well as the joy of what happens, because at no time more than a painful time do we live out of the depths of who we are instead of the shallows."[4] Are we willing to go through the pain of the wilderness and risk new life?

I still ponder that question when approaching a wilderness frontier. I still wonder if it wouldn't be better to cling to familiarity. As I ponder my dilemma, I hear Jesus's words anew: "I am the resurrection and the life. Though you die, yet shall you live. Do you believe this Marlena? Do you believe it?"

Jesus's question to me lingers in the air. Do I believe it? I want to believe it, Jesus. I want to believe that you created me at your own discretion and for your pleasure just the way I am. I've experienced how life comes to me every other time. Why shouldn't it come this time?

One of my great inspirations on this journey has been Macrina the Younger, the oldest sister in a large family of children who went on to influence church history. In some ways, I identify with her. Two of her brothers were Cappadocian Fathers—Basil the Great and Gregory of Nyssa. Macrina was renowned for her devotion to God and her simplicity, wisdom, and intellect. Among other things, Basil and Gregory were titans in the early church who played a crucial role in the formation of the doctrine of the Trinity, contributed to the Nicene Creed, and brilliantly argued against heresies. Author and Benedictine, Laura Swan tells us that Macrina's brothers "acknowledged her as the primary influence in their theological education" and due to her persuasion, they "finally embraced ascetic and monastic observance."[5]

Basil and Gregory weren't ashamed to acknowledge that their sister Macrina, a woman they and others venerated, was their theological teacher. Swan goes on to say that Basil is "credited as the founder of Eastern Monasticism, a movement that Macrina actually began."[6] Jesus's life and thought flowed from her into them and filtered down through church history to us today.

For some, it is no big deal to have a woman instruct them in the ways of God. But I've heard plenty of people, especially men, say that women cannot teach men from the Scriptures. Women cannot teach men theology. But isn't it true that any man who closely observes the life of a Christian woman is being taught theology? Didn't Jesus, even as a grown man, learn theology from his mother, Mary? She had a thing or two to teach him about faithfulness to God in the midst of difficulty. We cannot underestimate the role she played in forming him into the person he was. Jesus wouldn't be Jesus without Mary.

The assertion that women aren't permitted to use the Scriptures to instruct men has to be due to an ignorance of church history. If Basil and Gregory had been adherents of that type of theology, it is quite possible that we wouldn't have our doctrine of the Trinity, the Nicene Creed, the gift of monasticism, and much more. Christianity wouldn't be Christianity.

Women aren't the only ones who have been disregarded and rejected as bearers of the good news of the gospel—the good news of life in a world filled with death. In Jesus's day, little children weren't valued. They were disregarded, at the bottom of the totem pole, as it were. Maybe the youngest ones were considered a financial burden because they couldn't earn their keep. They were dependents.

When Jesus's disciples overlooked the little children who sought Jesus's time, attention, and affection and tried to shoo them away as if they were pesky flies, Jesus rebuked his disciples. "Let them come to me and be with me," Jesus said. "I will bless them" (see Matt. 19; Mark 10). There are many things we can learn from children, Jesus tells us. Most important is the lesson that to enter the kingdom of God we need to become like them.

Are there people we shoo away, people whom Jesus would welcome, people who are angelic messengers of the kingdom? God doesn't discriminate in his use of vessels, nor does he make mistakes in forming his vessels. He chooses whatever vessel he wills to deliver life to others. He chooses vessels we might not choose, such as women and little children—those considered by some as having little to no right to our attention.

We need to consider our prejudices. If we will not receive God's life because we don't prefer the vessel in which it comes, we may live an anemic Christian life or miss out on life altogether. We are limiting our capacity for life. People missed out on God's life in Jesus because of their preconceived notions of what the Messiah should be. We miss out on life because of our preconceived notions of where life should turn up.

Our desert experiences help us to let go of some of those preconceived notions. They teach us to receive the gift of life in its various forms. And they teach us that we can be and should be who God created us to be for the good of others. Jesus emerged from the desert very strong and with a clear sense of his identity and mission. He didn't allow naysayers to keep him from bringing God's life to others.

God the Father and God the Holy Spirit affirmed and confirmed Jesus's identity and his role at his baptism. John the Baptist, Peter, the other disciples (including the women who traveled with him and helped provide for him), his Word and his miracles, and all the others who believed in him also confirmed his identity. Today, we discern our roles in bringing life to others with the help of our communities. We will know that we are where we should be, doing what we should be, when our internal callings are confirmed by an external calling from our communities. God has made us at his discretion and for his pleasure, and he will fulfill his purposes for us, bringing about life through us, as we yield to him.

Life outside the Desert

Desert lessons aren't just essential for desert living. Jesus put into practice outside the desert what he learned in the desert. We too will emerge from God-bathed suffering with a clearer sense of identity and mission. It is impossible for us to have the kind of interactions with God we have in the wilderness and not come out transformed and fruitful people.

God redirects our lives through our desert experiences. God's life begets life in us in our wilderness experiences. And then his life, comingled with ours, flows out of us into the world. We experience streams of living water flowing from soil in our life that we previously believed was impenetrable and lifeless—soil as hard as rock. This is a miracle.

We come out of the desert with a healthy dose of self-forgetfulness and a firm resolve to serve God and others in love. Like Paul and the other apostles, we resolve to remember the poor and the afflicted. The desert has made us more compassionate toward those who are suffering, and so we seek to do what we can because we remember what it is like to despair and feel alone. Serving God becomes our pleasure. We live for the sake of God and others, for we have experienced the beauty, the brevity, and the fragility of life.

Givers of Life

We leave the wilderness grateful for life and grateful for those who have obeyed God in bringing us life. God has used many others to give us life. I would love to be able to trace the flow of God's life into me—my spiritual genealogy. It'd go way back, far back to the beginning of the known world.

God's life in me includes my family. My mom and dad have God's life in them, despite how much they've suffered. My dad has modeled the I'll-give-you-the-shirt-off-my-back kindness to others that is rubbing off on me. My mom has been an example of faithfulness and loyalty in the midst of great adversity. Abuelita, a devout Roman Catholic with a third-grade education, read her Bible daily and took me to Mass when she could. Looking back, I see she taught me the importance of regularly digesting Scripture. Uncle Craig gave me my first Bible and unknowingly sent me on a journey to discover what it means to fear the Lord. My husband, Shawn, has taught me more than anyone else what it means to be an integrity-filled, thinking, and servant-hearted disciple.

There are so many others. The faithful at Chapmanville Community Church, some of whom are no longer living, played a key role in loving me into the kingdom. I can still remember shaking in my boots, hoping and praying the German Shepherds standing guard on the porch of the elderly gentleman's white double-wide wouldn't chase after me and my siblings on our two-mile round-trip trek to and from church.

I wish I could name all the people and places and experiences that have given me life in Jesus's name—even in the wilderness. God has given me life through acquaintances and friends—those I've interacted with face-to-face. He has given me life through those whose words I've read or heard and through the testimony of Scripture. Life has come through those whose artwork I've absorbed in one form or another and through the witness of creation too. This universe is teeming with God's gracious life. It would be impossible to thank all those who have given us life in Jesus's name. All of us who are alive in the kingdom are intimately connected to one another. We are connected to both the living and the great cloud of witnesses who have gone before.

The Wilderness Life

We don't have to get stressed out about how exactly God will orchestrate his life in our lives and in our communities. We won't always know how life will manifest itself. If the wilderness has taught us anything, it has taught us that (1) God loves us dearly, (2) he is faithful in bringing about life, (3) he does it in his time, (4) he does it in the most unexpected ways, and (5) we can trust him.

C. S. Lewis reminds us that "we are metaphorically but in very truth, a Divine work of art, something God is making, and therefore something with which he will not be satisfied until it has a certain character."[7] Our loving Father's aim is that we be formed in the image of Jesus, his beloved Son. And so he will use our wilderness experiences to form us into a divine work of art that resembles Jesus Christ. God calls us to love and trust him throughout his life-making soul craft because he is loving and trustworthy. In the words of Frederick Buechner, "To be commanded to love God at all, let alone in the wilderness, is like being commanded to be well when we are sick, to sing for joy when we are dying of thirst, to run when our legs are broken. But this is the first and great commandment nonetheless. Even in the wilderness—especially in the wilderness—you shall love him."[8]

notes

foreword

1. http://www.dwillard.org/articles/artview.asp?artID=58.

chapter 1: the way of the desert and beautiful souls

1. John Stott, *The Cross of Christ* (Downers Grove, IL: InterVarsity, 1986), 320.

2. Audioslave, "Show Me How To Live," A-Z Lyrics Universe (website), http://www.azlyrics.com/lyrics/audioslave/showmehowtolive.html, accessed January 15, 2014.

3. St. John of the Cross, *Dark Night of the Soul*, ed. and trans. E. Allison Peers (New York: Image, 1990), 119.

4. N. T. Wright, *The Way of The Lord: Christian Pilgrimage Today* (Grand Rapids: Eerdmans, 1999), 36.

5. Eugene Peterson, *Leap over a Wall: Earthy Spirituality for Everyday Christians* (New York: HarperCollins, 1997), 73.

6. C. S. Lewis, *Mere Christianity* (New York: Macmillan, 1967), 94.

7. Bradley Nassif, "The Poverty of Love," *Christianity Today*, April 30, 2008, http://www.christianitytoday.com/ct/2008/may/11.34.html.

8. Peterson, *Leap over a Wall*, 73.

9. Robert Barry Leal, *Wilderness in the Bible: Toward a Theology of Wilderness* (New York: Peter Lang, 2004), 97–98.

chapter 2: who am i?

1. Rabbi Michael Leo Samuel, "What is the meaning of the names 'Esau' and 'Jacob'?," *Rabbi Michael Leo Samuel: Unorthodox Jewish reflections on the issue of our day* (blog), November 2009, http://rabbimichaelsamuel.com/2009/11/what-is-the-meaning-of-the-names-esau-and-jacob.

2. Ibid.

3. Ibid.

4. Edward F. Markquart, "Wrestling with God (Jacob)," Sermons from Seattle (website), http://www.sermonsfromseattle.com/series_c_wrestling_with_god.htm, accessed August 23, 2011.

5. Ibid.

6. Howard Thurman, *Jesus and the Disinherited* (Boston: Beacon Press, 1976), 28.

7. Thomas Merton, *New Seeds of Contemplation* (New York: New Directions, 1972), 34. http://www.fisheaters.com/srpdf/xThomasMertonNewSeedsOfContemplation.pdf, accessed December 22, 2013.

8. Dallas Willard, *The Divine Conspiracy: Rediscovering Our Hidden Life in God* (New York: HarperSanFrancisco, 1998), 62.

9. Greg Boyle, *Tattoos on the Heart: The Power of Boundless Compassion* (New York: Free Press, 2010), 22.

10. John Chryssavgis, *Light through Darkness: The Orthodox Tradition* (New York: Orbis Books, 2004), 65.

chapter 3: to your cell for goodness's sake

1. John Baillie, John T. McNeill, and Henry P. Van Dusen, eds., *The Library of Christian Classics*, vol. 12, *Western Asceticism*, trans., introduction, and notes Owen Chadwick (Philadelphia: Westminster Press, 1958), http://archive.org/stream /libraryofchristi008770mbp.

2. John L. Allen Jr., "Pope on Homosexuals: 'Who Am I to Judge?,'" *National Catholic Reporter*, July 29, 2013, http://ncronline.org/blogs/ncr-today/pope -homosexuals-who-am-i-judge.

3. Frederick Buechner, "Frederick Buechner," *Religion and Ethics News Weekly,* May 5, 2006, http://www.pbs.org/wnet/religionandethics/2006/05/05/may-5-2006 -frederick-buechner/15314/.

4. C. S. Lewis, preface to *Paradise Lost* as quoted in "Journaling with C. S. Lewis," explorefaith.org (website), 2005, http://www.explorefaith.org/tools/guided _journaling/guided_journaling_with_the_words_of_c.s._lewis.php.

5. C. S. Lewis, *The Voyage of the Dawn Treader*, The Chronicles of Narnia (New York: Collier Books, 1970), 91.

chapter 4: loved into resurrection

1. Nicholas Wolterstorff, *Until Justice and Peace Embrace* (Grand Rapids: Eerdmans, 1987), 69–70.

2. Ibid.

3. Greg Boyle, *Tattoos on the Heart: The Power of Boundless Compassion* (New York: Free Press, 2010), 44.

4. Jean Vanier, *From Brokenness to Community* (Mahwah, NJ: Paulist Press, 1992), 15.

5. Anthony de Mello, *The Way to Love: Meditations for Life* (New York: Image, 1992), 96.

6. Here I am not speaking of self-defense or physically defending innocent people from harm.

7. Dietrich Bonhoeffer, *Life Together* (New York: HarperSanFrancisco, 1954), 34.

8. Bernard of Clairvaux, "On Loving God," in *Bernard of Clairvaux: Selected Works*, The Classics of Western Spirituality Series (New York: Paulist Press, 1987), 179.

9. Bradley Nassif, "The Poverty of Love," *Christianity Today*, April 30, 2008, http://www.christianitytoday.com/ct/2008/may/11.34.html.

10. Dennis Okholm, *Monk Habits for Everyday People: Benedictine Spirituality for Protestants* (Grand Rapids: Brazos, 2007), 91.

11. James Bryan Smith, *The Good and Beautiful Life: Putting on the Character of Christ* (Downers Grove, IL: InterVarsity, 2009), 189.

12. Jan Johnson, *Invitation to the Jesus Life: Experiments in Christlikeness* (Colorado Springs: NavPress, 2008), 19.

chapter 5: testing and temptation

1. Blaise Pascal, *Pensees*, www.gutenberg.org/files/18269/18269-h/18269-h.htm, accessed December 26, 2013.

2. *Hannah and Her Sisters*, directed by Woody Allen (Los Angeles: Orion Pictures, 1986).

3. C. S. Lewis, *Reflection on the Psalms* (New York: Harvest Book, 1964), 28–32.

4. Shawn and I spoke up on behalf of our friend and others who became targets. We suffered greatly because of it. Yet we wouldn't change a thing. In chapter 6, I describe what happened after we refused to remain silent about the injustices we witnessed firsthand.

5. Evagrius Ponticus, *The Praktikos and Chapters on Prayer*, trans. John Eudes Bamberger, OSCO (Trappist, KY: Cistercian Publications, 1972), 18.

6. Ibid.

7. C. S. Lewis, *The Problem of Pain* (New York: HarperOne, 1996), 111.

8. John Paul Sartre, "No Exit," http://archive.org/stream/NoExit/NoExit_djvu .txt, accessed December 30, 2013.

9. Lewis, *Problem of Pain*, 111.

10. Flannery O'Connor, *Flannery O'Connor: Spiritual Writings*, ed. Robert Ellsberg (Maryknoll, NY: Orbis Books, 2003), 75, emphasis added.

11. St. Macarius, as quoted by Father Stephen, "The Treasures of the Heart," *Glory to God* (radio program), Ancient Faith Radio, December 5, 2009, http:// www.ancientfaith.com/podcasts/freeman/the_treasures_of_the_heart.

12. John Arnold, *Life Conquers Death: Meditations on the Garden, the Cross, and the Tree of Life* (Grand Rapids: Zondervan, 2007), 118.

13. Ibid.

14. Lewis, *Problem of Pain*, 46.

chapter 6: careless in the care of God

1. Martin Luther King Jr., *I Have a Dream: Writings and Speeches That Changed the World*, cited at Goodreads (website), http://www.goodreads.com/quotes/6407 -our-lives-begin-to-end-the-day-we-become-silent, accessed December 30, 2013.

2. Fr. John Jay Hughes, "That My Joy May Be in You," *Now You Know Media Blog*, May 7, 2012, http://homilies.nowyouknowmedia.com/that-my-joy-may-be -in-you.

3. Carlo Carretto, cited in *A Guide to Prayer for Ministers and Other Servants*, ed. Rueben P. Job and Norman Shawchuck (Nashville: Upper Room Books, 1983), 19.

4. Frederick Buechner, *Telling Secrets: A Memoir* (New York: HarperSan-Francisco, 1991), 26.

5. Laura Swan, *The Forgotten Desert Mothers: Sayings, Lives, and Stories of Early Christian Women* (New York: Paulist Press, 2001), 21.

chapter 7: waiting around for God

1. Here I play with the title of Eugene Peterson's classic work: *A Long Obedience in the Same Direction: Discipleship in an Instant Society* (Downers Grove, IL: InterVarsity, 1980).

2. Brother Lawrence, *Practice of the Presence of God: The Best Rule of Holy Life*, Christian Classics Ethereal Library (website), http://www.ccel.org/ccel/lawrence /practice.iii.iii.html, accessed April 14, 2013.

3. Andrew Murray, *Waiting on God* (Radford, VA: Wilder Publications, 2008), 7.

4. Jean-Pierre de Caussade, *The Joy of Full Surrender* (Orleans, MA: Paraclete Press, 2008).

5. Karen Swallow-Prior, *Booked: Literature in the Soul of Me* (New York: T. S. Poetry Press, 2012), 91.

6. Portions of this section appeared in the April 2013 issue of the CRC's *The Banner*. Reprinted with permission.

7. Kathleen Norris, *Acedia and Me: A Marriage, Monks, and a Writer's Life* (New York: Riverhead Books, 2008), 45.

8. Evagrius Ponticus, *The Praktikos and Chapters on Prayer*, trans. John Eudes Bamberger, OSCO (Trappist, KY: Cistercian Publications, 1972), 18.

9. This is the topic of de Caussade's work, *The Joy of Full Surrender*.

10. Mark Mallett, "The Sacrament of the Present Moment," *Mark Mallet: Spiritual Food for Thought* (blog), February 2, 2007, http://www.markmallett .com/blog/the-sacrament-of-the-present-moment/.

11. Norris, *Acedia and Me*, 111.

chapter 8: the death of a dream

1. Telephone conversation with David Matthew Mills, June 26, 2013.

2. Ibid.

3. "The Frank Laubach Story," Laubach Literacy of Ventura County, Inc. (website), http://www.laubachventura.org/about/the-frank-laubach-story.html, accessed July 15, 2013.

4. Ibid.

5. Frank C. Laubach Collection, Syracuse University Libraries, http://library .syr.edu/digital/guides/l/laubach_coll.htm, accessed July 15, 2013.

6. Ibid.

chapter 9: the God who sees me

1. Jean Vanier, *From Brokenness to Community* (Mahwah, NJ: Paulist Press, 1992), 16.
2. Frederick Buechner, *Beyond Words*, quoted in "Living Spiritual Teachers Project: Frederick Buechner," Spirituality and Practice (website), http://www.spirituality andpractice.com/teachers/teachers.php?id=215&g=1, accessed August 22, 2013.
3. Dallas Willard, *The Divine Conspiracy: Rediscovering Our Hidden Life in God* (New York: HarperSanFrancisco, 1998), 188.
4. Ibid.
5. Henri M. Nouwen, *Letters to Marc about Jesus: Living a Spiritual Life in a Material World* (New York: HarperCollins, 2009), 72.
6. Ibid.
7. Ibid.
8. J. R. R. Tolkien, *The Return of the King* (New York: Ballantine Books, 1965), 190.

chapter 10: weak and wise athletes of God

1. Dietrich Bonhoeffer, *The Cost of Discipleship* (New York: Simon and Schuster, 1959), 89.
2. John Chryssavgis, *Light through Darkness: The Orthodox Tradition* (New York: Orbis Books, 2004), 72.
3. Miroslav Volf, *Exclusion and Embrace: A Theological Explanation of Identity, Otherness, and Reconciliation* (Nashville: Abingdon, 1996), 105.
4. Mother Teresa, Goodreads (website), http://www.goodreads.com/quotes /9401, accessed June 20, 2013.
5. Henri Nouwen, *In the Name of Jesus: Reflections on Christian Leadership* (New York: Crossroad, 1989), 76.
6. Ibid.
7. Ibid., 77.

chapter 11: trembling in fear and adoration

1. "The Deadliest Tsunami in History?," *National Geographic News*, January 7, 2005, http://news.nationalgeographic.com/news/2004/12/1227_041226_tsunami .html.
2. Thomas Aquinas, "The Gift of Fear (Second Part of the Second Part Question 19)," in *Summa Theologica*, http://www.newadvent.org/summa/3019.htm#article6, accessed July 23, 2013.
3. *My Utmost for his Highest* is the title of Oswald Chambers's classic devotional book.
4. Used with permission from Judy Douglass.
5. Henri Nouwen, *Spiritual Formation: Following the Movements of the Spirit*, ed. Michael J. Christensen and Rebecca J. Laird (New York: HarperCollins, 2010), 83.
6. Jo Kadlecek, *Fear: A Spiritual Navigation* (Colorado Springs: Waterbrook Press, 2001), 91.

7. Ibid., 113.

8. Greg Boyle, *Tattoos on the Heart: The Power of Boundless Compassion* (New York: Free Press, 2010), 22.

chapter 12: children in the kingdom of God

1. John Arnold, *Life Conquers Death: Meditations on the Garden, the Cross, and the Tree of Life* (Grand Rapids: Zondervan, 2007), 51.

2. Here I do not advocate staying in physically, sexually, or emotionally abusive situations. Please get whatever help you need to get out.

3. Gregory of Nyssa, "On the Lord's Prayer," as quoted in the introduction to Kathleen Norris, *The Quotidian Mysteries: Laundry, Liturgy, and "Women's Work"* (New York: Paulist Press, 1998).

4. G. K. Chesterton, *Orthodoxy* (Colorado Springs: Shaw Books, 1994), 84.

5. Ibid.

6. Gerard Manley Hopkins, "As Kingfishers Catch Fire," Poetry Foundation (website), http://www.poetryfoundation.org/poem/173654, accessed January 5, 2014.

7. James Bryan Smith, *The Good and Beautiful Life: Putting on the Character of Christ* (Downers Grove, IL: InterVarsity, 2009), 181.

8. Jo Kadlecek, *Fear: A Spiritual Navigation* (Colorado Springs: Waterbrook Press, 2001), 90.

chapter 13: a human being fully alive

1. Francis of Assisi, "All Creatures of Our God and King," 1225, trans. William Draper, 1910, found in the *Psalter Hymnal* of the Christian Reformed Church, 431.

2. Mark Dimmitt, "Predicting Desert Wildflower Blooms: The Science behind the Spectacle," Arizona-Sonora Desert Museum, http://www.desertmuseum.org/programs/flw_predicting.php, accessed August 17, 2013.

3. Frederick Buechner, *Secrets in the Dark: A Life in Sermons* (New York: HarperSanFrancisco, 2006), 216.

4. Ibid.

5. Laura Swan, *The Forgotten Desert Mothers: Sayings, Lives, and Stories of Early Christian Women* (Mahwah, NJ: Paulist Press, 2001), 129.

6. Ibid.

7. C. S. Lewis, *The Problem of Pain* (New York: HarperOne, 1996), 34.

8. Frederick Buechner, *A Room Called Remember*, cited at Goodreads (website), http://www.goodreads.com/quotes/33456-to-be-commanded-to-love-god-at-all-let-alone, accessed August 17, 2013.